[extra] ORDINARY
women

Published by
The Bible Reading Fellowship
First Floor, Elsfield Hall
15–17 Elsfield Way, Oxford OX2 8FG
ISBN 1 84101 235 1

First published 2003
1 3 5 7 9 10 8 6 4 2

Acknowledgments
Unless otherwise stated, scripture quotations are taken from The New
Revised Standard Version of the Bible, Anglicized Edition, copyright ©
1989, 1995 by the Division of Christian Education of the National
Council of the Churches of Christ in the USA, and are used by
permission. All rights reserved.

Scripture quotations from The Revised Standard Version of the Bible,
copyright © 1946, 1952, 1971 by the Division of Christian Education of
the National Council of the Churches of Christ in the United Sates of
America, and are used by permission. All rights reserved.

Extracts reprinted with the permission of Simon & Schuster from *The New
Testament in Modern English*, Revised Edition, translated by J.B. Phillips.
Copyright © 1958, 1960, 1972 by J.B. Phillips.

A catalogue record for this book is available from the British Library

Printed and bound in Great Britain by
Bookmarque, Croydon

[extra]ORDINARY
Reflections for women on Bible-based living
women

CLARE blake

To my Mum, Rosie, and my spiritual Mum, Joyce.
With love and thanks to two Extraordinary Women!

Acknowledgments

Behind every book there is a whole host of people supporting and encouraging—a bit like a circus balancing act!

For *(Extra)Ordinary Women*, special mention must go to Jill, who printed my very first article and suggested the book project.

To the Mothers' Union, who gave positive feedback on my devotional writing and gave me the incentive to press on.

To Naomi, Lisa and the BRF team, who not only publish but pray a book through.

To Wendy V, who spared time from a hectic schedule to write not only the foreword but words of encouragement.

To my family, writing friends, the home church in Honiton, and Christian friends throughout the country, including two special e-mail friends, Wendy B and Sheila, who gave constant prayer and support and fanned the flame when it burned low.

And of course to Steve, David and Peter who have empathized, sympathized, criticized when necessary and served as a sounding-board for ideas—sometimes at 5am! Without them this book could not have been written.

And to the One who made it all possible!

Contents

Missing pieces

Love—a tender plant

Wings like an eagle

Foreword

The word of God is what guides, teaches and motivates Christian women. For many of us, life is a blur, and it is not always easy to give time to reading and praying. A book like this helps us to centre our thoughts, and can be used perhaps while travelling to work on the train, or while snatching a cup of coffee mid-morning.

It is a collection of meditations set around the ordinary things of life which an ordinary Christian woman encounters. I imagine that Clare has accumulated these thoughts over a long period of time, and maybe honed them while ironing, weeding the garden or cleaning the bathroom! She writes about such things as jigsaw puzzles, traffic jams, building sites and quarrelling children. Most of us observe these things in passing, and get irritated or mildly interested or momentarily intrigued; but Clare has learnt to go through life with a discerning eye and a hearing ear. Her observations go beyond the superficial and she has turned minor incidents into learning experiences, and moments of reflection into nuggets of wisdom. It is as if time is recorded on video tape and she has focused on rich moments and made still photos out of them.

This is a book to dip into, to take on a weekend away, to keep in your handbag or at your bedside. It will also be a treasure to give to your friends. The truth distilled here has the potential to change ordinary women into extraordinary women, those whose lives are enriched, purified and changed by the word of God.

Wendy Virgo

Introduction

Have you ever felt that women in the Bible were superstars, somehow extra specially blessed by God, and that this is why their names are recorded in scripture? 'Of course they must have had really special qualities for God to use them,' you might sigh. 'Not like me—I'm just ordinary.' But actually, when we look at these women more closely, we don't find this to be the case at all.

When I look at Martha complaining to Jesus that she's been left to do everything singlehanded and why doesn't Mary help—can't she see how much there is to do?—I get a sense of, 'Been there, done that!' Or what about the mother of James and John trying to get the best places in heaven for her sons? Have you ever wanted to push your kids into the limelight?

The more I look at these women, the more I realize that they experienced the same tensions, hopes and fears and struggled with the same universal feminine dilemmas as the rest of us. And if God can use a Mary or a Martha, a Sarah, a Leah or a Rebekah in all their human frailty, then what's to stop him using me?

God looks beyond our failings and weaknesses to the women we will become as we learn to follow him, step by faltering step. To him, each of us is a 'one off' with a unique combination of personality and giftings. In his eyes there are no 'ordinary' women—only 'extra-ordinary' women—and he loves us to bits!

WHO, ME, LORD?

❖

Who, me, Lord?

It was just a normal day in Mary's home as she busied herself about her daily chores. Perhaps she was spinning, or baking bread for the evening meal.

However, this was one day that Mary was never going to forget. Just having an angel appear was extraordinary enough. It certainly wasn't an everyday happening in the small town of Nazareth where she lived. She had never met anyone like him before.

But when he spoke, what he said was even more surprising: 'Greetings, favoured one! The Lord is with you.'

Surely he couldn't mean her? She was just a humble village girl. 'Favoured one!' What did it all mean? Mary probably wondered at first whether there had been some mistake. 'Who, me, Lord?'

God delights in taking uncertain people who cannot believe they have been chosen—'Who, me, Lord?'—and transforming them into radical men and women of God.

It was God who found Gideon hiding from the Midianites, threshing wheat in a wine press, and said to him, 'The Lord is with you, you mighty warrior!' (Judges 6:12).

At the time, Gideon must have felt embarrassed and confused. Here he was, skulking away in fear for his life. Nothing could be further from the behaviour of a mighty warrior. 'Who, me, Lord? No, you've got the wrong person!'

God makes no mistakes, however. He doesn't choose people according to worldly values. He doesn't really care whether you have good qualifications or none at all, whether you are rich and famous or poor and nondescript. He looks at your heart response to him, and very often it is those who are weakest in the world's eyes that he can use most because they realize how much they need to depend on him.

Paul reassures us in 1 Corinthians 1:26–27 that of those responding to God's call, 'not many of you were wise by human standards, not many were powerful, not many were of noble birth. But God chose what is foolish in the world to shame the wise; God chose what is weak in the world to shame the strong.'

When you look at the first followers of Jesus you realize what a motley crew they were. They included loud-mouthed Peter who was continually getting into hot water, a reformed prostitute and even a future traitor—not ideal candidates for the job!

All of these people probably thought when Jesus called them, 'Who, me, Lord? But you don't know what my life has been like. I've made so many mistakes. I'm really not worthy to be your follower at all!'

We can be just the same. We've probably all experienced the gentle prodding of the Holy Spirit to do something for Jesus:

- talk to that other mum at the school gate
- begin teaching a Sunday School group
- pray out loud in the midweek meeting
- hold a coffee morning for Third World relief

The problem is that very often these things, small though they might seem in comparison to Gideon leading God's army or Moses' confrontations with Pharaoh (Exodus 5—11), can have just as much power to make us shake in our shoes.

We may feel inadequate for the task ahead of us and may be tempted to argue with God. 'You want me to do this for you, Lord? Surely you don't mean me. I'd make a total mess of it! Why don't you choose Ruth or Jane or Grace? I'm sure they'd make a much better job of it. I'd only let you down.'

I hope we wouldn't behave like Jonah. He tried to run away from the task God gave him, and it took several days in the belly of a giant fish to bring him to his senses and convince him that the right course of action was to obey God.

Mary's response was totally different.

Probably no one else has ever been given such an awesome task to fulfil—to be the mother of God's Son. Mary must have felt completely out of her depth. She wasn't even married and risked the stigma of public disapproval and even the loss of her fiancé.

Yet she was able to face the task before her with grace and joy: 'Here am I, the servant of the Lord; let it be with me according to your word' (Luke 1:38).

When God asks us to do something for him, we may whisper faint-heartedly, 'Who, me, Lord?'

Jesus just looks at us with such love in his eyes. He knows exactly what we're like—all our strengths, our weaknesses, our worries, our fears. He knows us inside out, warts and all.

'Yes, you, daughter,' he replies. 'Come, follow me.'

❖

Small cogs

Do you ever have the feeling that you are just a small cog in a very big wheel?

Perhaps you are a mum with young children, who can't remember how it feels to be able to talk to friends for a solid hour without constant interruptions—nowadays you've almost forgotten how to string a sentence together!

Or maybe you work in a place where job satisfaction is minimal and you feel undervalued as a person, just part of the office furniture.

The little maid in 2 Kings 5 was right at the bottom of the social pecking order of her time. In fact, she was so insignificant in the terms of her culture that we don't even know her name. All we know is that she had been captured as a young girl and taken away from her home in Israel.

She was alone in a land whose ways were foreign to her. Her family was lost—almost certainly she would never see them again. Perhaps they had even been killed in the same raid when she was captured.

She was no longer free to do what she wanted when she wanted. Instead she had to obey the commands of a master and a mistress and live surrounded by those who were enemies of her people. In fact, her master was not just anyone—he was one of the most brilliant military commanders on the opposite side.

He was also a very sick man, plagued with leprosy.

The little maid had good cause to hate him: he had taken her away from everything she loved. She had reason to fear him too: he worshipped strange heathen idols instead of the one true God whom she knew. How easy it would have been for the maid to become bitter and resentful in her captivity. Hadn't she lost everything?

There was one thing she hadn't lost, however. She still possessed the most important thing of all—her faith in God—and she knew that her God, the God of Israel, had the power to heal Naaman in his desperate need.

Many in her situation would have been tempted to withhold the information. Let Naaman ask the foreign gods he worshipped for help! Why should an enemy of Israel be saved? Let him suffer!

The maid reacted differently. In spite of her captivity, she had not become bitter and twisted. Although technically Naaman was the enemy, she reached out to him as another human being needing to know the sovereign love of God.

You can sense the quiet faith of this young girl as she speaks to her mistress. 'If only my lord were with the prophet who is in Samaria! He would cure him of his leprosy' (2 Kings 5:3). She had no doubt at all that the God in whom she trusted would heal Naaman.

I am sure that when Naaman's wife first told him what their serving maid had said, he was tempted to dismiss it. Wealthy and influential, he would certainly have spent time and money consulting the best doctors he could find. The little maid—she was a nobody! Why should he, the mighty Naaman, take her advice?

But there must have been something in her that won him over. As she served them day after day in the most menial of tasks, something shone through that convinced him that this young woman knew what she was talking about, and made him prepared to take the step of trusting her.

In the eyes of Naaman's household, the maid was insignificant, but in God's eyes she had a key part to play.

What would have happened if she had been so overawed by the high status of her employer that she hadn't dared to speak up and bring God's perspective? What if she'd thought, 'He's my boss—how can I possibly speak to him? He'll never listen to me!'

The maid knew that position didn't matter. She knew that, far from being a nobody, she was a Somebody because God loved her. She looked beyond the limitations of her circumstances and continued acting as a child of God in the situation in which she found herself.

Because of her obedience, Naaman, one of the greatest leaders in the land, did end up being healed; but more than this, he met with the living God in whom his servant believed and trusted, and his whole life was radically changed.

We should never feel disqualified from serving God by what we do.

It really doesn't matter whether we hold an important position or whether in the world's eyes we are of no value at all, spending most of the day at the kitchen sink.

The fact is that God is with us wherever we are—at home, at work, in our leisure pursuits, in every moment of every day. Just as he did with the unnamed maid, God can work through us and change the lives of those around us—if we allow him to.

✜

Free gift enclosed

As a family, we are absolute suckers for a free gift. Show us a cereal packet with a novelty item enclosed and we'll put it in the shopping trolley. Our home is littered with little plastic figures of cartoon characters and football heroes.

Of course the gifts vary in quality. Some are cheap and easily broken while others are still proudly displayed on shelves in the children's bedrooms many years later.

When God created us, part of the package was the inclusion of exciting gifts, unique to us and absolutely free of charge. Just as the goods manufacturer envisages an excited child discovering the sealed packet and ripping it open to discover what is hidden inside, so God waits expectantly for his children to begin to explore and use what he has hidden away within us, the seeds of his creativity waiting to explode into new and vibrant growth.

The free gifts that God gives us are not static and lifeless like the novelty gimmicks given away as incentives to buy certain products. He does not intend us to place them on a shelf to look at, occasionally getting them down for a quick dust before replacing them in their original position.

The gifts given to us are gifts that actually grow and expand—living gifts. But in order to grow, they must be used.

When Elisha told the widow in 2 Kings 4 to bring out what she had in her house, all she could contribute was one jar of oil. She probably wondered what on earth she was supposed to do with it. One jar of oil—it didn't amount to much.

However, when Elisha told her to fetch as many empty vessels as she could, she did what he said. 'Pour until the first one is full and then keep pouring,' commanded the prophet and, to her amazement, the oil from the one small jar she already had began to flow and kept flowing until she had filled every pot full to the brim.

The talent we possess may seem very small and insignificant to us—

just one jar of oil, hardly worth using at all. Perhaps it would be better to store it until some later date. After all, the oil will keep.

It is true that the oil will remain in the jar, but it is of no use while it is being contained and may eventually lose its freshness. Only as we begin to exercise the talent(s) that God has given us will the fresh oil begin to flow.

God expects us to use the gifts he gives us. How would you feel if you'd spent hours walking round the shops to choose a gift for your best friend, carefully selecting an item that you felt would really suit her personality, and that she would be thrilled to receive, and then she put it away without even opening it?

Yet how often do we do that with a talent that God has given us? Perhaps we lack confidence, afraid that we might make a fool of ourselves if we launch out in a new direction rather than staying in the old comfortable rut.

Or perhaps we start something new and then lose heart, giving up. Sometimes we need to persevere in seeking to pursue a particular area of gifting.

The widow might well have felt tempted to stop halfway through her task, leaving some jars half filled or even empty. Probably the jar of oil was quite heavy and her arm muscles were beginning to ache, but she knew that God could only multiply what she had if she did her part too.

The amazing thing is that as we start to move out and use the gifting he has given us—as we begin to shape the words of a poem, cook a wonderful meal for guests, lead a Bible study that inspires others, create a beautiful garden that refreshes those who walk in it, or build a friendship with a lonely neighbour—we will see our gifts grow and develop, and not only will they bless us, they will bless others too.

Do you know that God loves creativity? You only have to look around you to see the hand of the master craftsman at work. Have you ever noticed, for example, how many shades of green there are? And why so many types of cloud? Look at the giraffe, the zebra, the duck-billed platypus. Aren't they glorious, aren't they fun?

God wants us to be the most creative people on planet Earth, full of ideas and enthusiasm, ready to try out new things, to inspire, to excite, to ignite!

And as we fill each jar to the brim with the fresh oil of the free gifts with which he supplies us, he'll provide another—and another—and another!

❖

Models / rôle models

Women's magazines are full of them—tall, willowy figures draped in the latest fashions, posing provocatively, immaculately made-up faces pouting.

The glossy adverts tantalize us with seductive promises: 'After four weeks the appearance of wrinkles and lines will have diminished by up to 69 per cent. Your skin will be firmer and younger looking.'

Wear this perfume and handsome men will shower you with bouquets. Use this lipstick for a kissable mouth. Wear this outfit and look like a million dollars. Buy me, buy me, buy me—if you do, you will instantly become more attractive!

It's easy to absorb the subtle underlying message that all you have to do is to dye your hair the right shade of blonde, achieve the right figure through exercise, wear the right perfume and choose the latest fashions to wear, and the world will be your oyster.

This is not just a modern problem. For centuries, women have been concerned with their outward appearance and have felt that the way they look dictates how successful they are in life.

So what hope is there for those of us who look in the mirror and see, let's admit it, a rather less than perfect image?

Plenty! There is nothing wrong with making the most of the looks that God has given us but we should be spending far more time on developing our inner beauty as godly women.

'Beauty is only skin deep,' says the old proverb, and the Bible agrees. Proverbs 11:22 puts it very succinctly: 'Like a gold ring in a pig's snout is a beautiful woman without good sense.' It's not a very flattering image!

Beauty is of little value to God unless a beautiful character goes with it. 1 Peter 3:3 says, 'Do not adorn yourselves outwardly by braiding your hair, and by wearing gold ornaments or fine clothing; rather, let your adornment be the inner self with the lasting beauty of a gentle and quiet spirit, which is very precious in God's sight.'

There is much more to being a beautiful woman of God than slavishly following fashion trends.

In sport, those who want to make their mark will often spend hours studying the techniques of past and present players in order to improve their level of skill.

In many other areas, such as art, music or politics, the same holds true. It is accepted that in order to learn, you model yourself on others who have passed that way before.

You also learn different things from different people. As an art student, you may at one point be studying the quality of light expressed in an Old Master like Rembrandt; and, the next moment, be admiring the jagged innovation of a Picasso.

We can learn so much from other Christian women and save ourselves many mistakes in the process. In the Bible we can study Ruth and her faithful loyalty to Naomi, or spend time with the woman in Proverbs 31, marvelling at the way she successfully interweaves all the different strands of her life.

Then there are past and present women of faith who inspire us with their passion for God—women like Susannah Wesley, Catherine Booth, Amy Carmichael, Mother Teresa and Jackie To Pullinger. The list is endless.

In our own churches, too, there are women who simply radiate God's character. Author Joyce L. Heatherley calls people like these 'balcony people'. They are people who inspire us with their desire to get close to God and serve him whatever the cost, becoming more like him in the process.

Of course our ultimate rôle model is the Lord Jesus himself. Each day he draws us on, teaching us more about himself. The amazing thing is that as we walk close to him an astonishing transformation takes place. It no longer matters what we look like on the outside—if our nose is much too large, or we suffer from middle-age spread, or whether or not our complexion is wrinkle-free. His beauty shines through us and makes us beautiful too!

✤

One anothering

''S mine!' announced the little boy at playgroup fiercely whenever another child came anywhere near him, clutching the bright red toy sports car possessively. He didn't seem to realize how much more fun he could have had if he'd played cars with someone else. No, he preferred not to play with it at all, rather than risk someone else touching it.

In complete contrast, the same playgroup would show you the natural givers, children who would take toys and give them to others, even sharing alternate bites of a soggy biscuit with a friend at break time.

God loves it when we stop acting selfishly and start reaching out to others, sharing our lives with them. We were never intended to live in holy isolation. God loves people and he wants us to love them as well.

Love is one of the great hallmarks of a Christian. John 13:35 quotes the words of Jesus, 'By this everyone will know that you are my disciples, if you have love one for another.'

The phrases 'one for another' and 'one another' appear over and over again in the Bible:

- 'Therefore confess your sins to one another, and pray for one another, so that you may be healed' (James 5:16).
- 'Love one another deeply from the heart' (1 Peter 1:22).
- 'Serve one another with whatever gift each of you has received' (1 Peter 4:10).
- 'Be kind to one another, tenderhearted, forgiving one another' (Ephesians 4:32).

For some of us, 'one anothering' is something we learn slowly and painfully; to others it is second nature. I think that Dorcas, who was raised miraculously from the dead in Acts 9:36–41, was one of the latter.

When we first hear of Dorcas, she has just died. The apostle Peter is summoned by the disciples to Joppa and, on arrival, finds a group of widows weeping over garments that Dorcas made for them.

Why such a fuss? Was it just the fact that Dorcas had provided them with free clothes that made these women so sad? I don't think so. The real reason these handmade clothes were so important was that every stitch reflected her love for them as individuals.

What does it take to become a 'one anotherer' like Dorcas?

We probably all like to think that we have a serving heart. Of course we're only too willing to help others if it doesn't clash with something else we've already planned to do, and doesn't cost too much in terms of time, energy, or money.

How do we feel if we're asked to do something behind the scenes? Do we want to get involved only if everyone knows what we're doing and appreciates our efforts?

Would we tackle a task so enthusiastically if we knew that our contribution would never be recognized or acknowledged, if nobody else knew what we were doing?

I don't believe that Dorcas thought in terms of whether or not what she did was worth the effort. She just did it anyway. Unfortunately we often do things for others out of a sense of duty, because we know it's the right thing to do as a Christian, acting with our head rather than our heart.

The response of the mourners showed that Dorcas was not like this. Dorcas gave them far more than just a gift of clothing. She gave them love, like the Lord and Master she so faithfully followed.

Have you ever thrown a stone into the middle of a pond and watched the way that ripples spread out from it in ever-widening circles? Our every action and word has a knock-on effect like that, either positive or negative.

I am sure that the simple way in which Dorcas demonstrated her love and care for those about her was noticed by others in the community. I can imagine the scene in the local marketplace.

'What a beautiful new robe, Hannah!'

'Thank you, Abigail.'

'I especially like the colour. It matches your eyes perfectly. Where did you buy it?'

'Oh, I didn't buy it.'

'Well, where did you get it from?'

'Actually, Dorcas made it for me.'

'Oh, you paid her to make up the material?'

'No, she just gave it to me.'

'Well, why did she do that?'

'I think she just likes to do it. She's a Christian, you know.'

Dorcas didn't blind people with her grasp of theology. She didn't get up on a pedestal and preach. She didn't need to. She simply took the skills she had and used them for the benefit of those among whom she lived. The clothes she made with such loving care were just a symbol of a deeper concern for those around her, a love that spoke far louder than words.

Jesus, of course, loved to 'one another'. He was not just called the Son of God but the Son of Man. Everywhere he went, he picked out people who were lonely, rejected or outcasts and gave them his loving acceptance.

Even when he was about to eat his very last meal with his disciples, Jesus reached out to those around him in love, emphasizing how special they were to him.

He could easily have commanded the disciples to bow down and worship him. After all, he was the Son of God, sinless, pure and holy. Instead Jesus took a towel and began to wash and dry the feet of his followers—the task of a servant (John 13:4–5).

True 'one anothering' is not easy. It will put us out, because to 'one another' we need to step outside our comfort zone.

We cannot just project loving thoughts into the air and trust that somehow people will sense them. We have to get our hands dirty and become actively involved with those around us.

'One anothering' reveals the heart of God in action, a love that doesn't say 'Me first' but 'You first'—love not on a pedestal, but on its knees.

✤

School reports

The big brown envelope lying on the desk contains a very important document—the end-of-year school report. The piece of paper inside sums up in a few telling phrases what we have achieved—or not achieved—in the preceding months. In just a few more hours, all will be revealed, our strengths and weaknesses graded and evaluated.

Do you remember that feeling in the pit of your stomach, watching your parents reading intently and waiting to see whether they reacted with joy or disappointment?

All of us have things that we are naturally good at and it's not too difficult to do well in those subjects. But then there are the ones where you struggle and the ones where, quite honestly, you haven't the foggiest idea what the teacher is trying to communicate.

Maths was like that for me. However hard I tried to make sense of figures, their meaning completely evaded me. They might as well have been Egyptian hieroglyphs as far as I was concerned!

My reports were studded with comments from the maths teacher like, '*Constant* application is needed to grasp mathematical concepts' or 'Continues to be weak. Greater effort needed.'

It's just as well we don't have reports for our progress in the Christian life. Can you imagine it?

Prayer:	Must concentrate harder and avoid distractions, e.g. shopping lists, children's behaviour, setting the video for that gardening programme etc.
Bible Study:	*Regular* application needed—must apply what has been read. Missed several days last week.
Love:	Lost temper with children—and husband! Did, however, help neighbour—well done!
Hospitality:	'Too tired'—not really a valid excuse.
Peace:	Has been seriously lacking in past weeks. House more like a war zone. See me!

Fortunately God is not like a vigilant headmaster constantly marking our progress and keeping a record of our (many) failures. If we do slip up and do something wrong, all we have to do is to come to him, confess it, and ask for forgiveness. I love Isaiah 43:25: 'I, I am he who blots out your transgressions for my own sake, and I will not remember your sins.'

Our sins are not just filed away in some storeroom to confront us at some later date—they are totally erased from the record!

I never really did get to grips with maths and was very relieved when I moved on to A' levels and could leave fractions, decimals and equations behind me at long last.

In the school of Christian life, however, things we find difficult often become real strengths as we mature and grow.

I've heard it said that God loves us totally just as we are—but loves us too much to leave us as we are! Haven't you found that to be true? God gives us no peace if we try to gloss over character flaws.

Have you ever felt God's hand on you for change? Perhaps you pray for the gift of patience and then suddenly find yourself swamped by a series of events that test you to the limit.

'What on earth are you doing, Lord?' you cry.

'I am putting you in situations where you will develop the character qualities you need to grow. Trust me,' he replies.

God doesn't need a report to assess our progress. He is vitally interested in us as whole people and will work with us on our weaknesses. He turns a wronged and bitter woman like Leah into one who can praise him for his goodness (Genesis 29:35).

He turns a cynic like Sarai into a believer who laughs with joy as she sees his promises fulfilled in her life (Genesis 21:6).

He turns hate into love, resentment into forgiveness, shyness into boldness.

God knows what is best for each of his daughters and in the loving school of his discipline we learn from the beloved teacher that those things we find hardest become possible when we lean on him and trust him to carry us through.

❖

Building site

When our children were younger, they loved to visit a new property development nearby and watch the builders at work. Walking from one end of the site to the other was a fascinating experience. At first there were houses much like anywhere else, with curtains hanging at the windows and cars parked in the driveways, but a little further down the road the scene changed.

Here the houses were ready for people to move into but still empty, with 'For Sale' posters displayed. Then came the exciting bit, for just a few hundred yards away building was still in progress.

As we stood looking at the chaos and dust of the building site, it was hard to imagine that what was going on here could ever result in the immaculate buildings standing at the top of the road.

It was a complete mess—an area of weedy ground littered with piles of bricks and sacks of cement, with clouds of dust everywhere. And noise—drills and hammers and shouting and a constant deafening roar of bulldozers and lorries trundling back and forth.

What we were looking at could have been anything. Although all the materials needed for a building had been brought together ready for use, there was nothing visible to show what was finally going to be constructed there.

A haphazard collection of bricks is not a house, even though it is true that a house is constructed largely of bricks. There has to be something else.

Before construction work begins, a detailed plan is drawn up which tells the builder what to do with the bricks and whether he will be building a patio, a wall or a complete building.

As onlookers, we knew that these builders were building houses, but we still had no idea what kind of houses. Would they be semi-detached or detached, with single or double garage, three or four bedrooms?

However, the builders knew exactly what they were doing and how the finished building would look, because the architect's plan showed the exact dimensions and what to put where.

If we had been shown the architect's drawing, it would probably have just seemed like a sketched outline on a piece of paper, but the construction workers were already familiar with the architect's instructions. They had followed them before so they were able to convert these pen strokes into three-dimensional form.

They knew which lines symbolized windows or doors and that a certain small marked area on the paper meant that the architect wanted them to include an en-suite bathroom or utility room.

In our Christian lives we sometimes pile up isolated heaps of building materials and imagine that somehow, just by having them, we are in the process of building something.

'Yes, these are the building materials of my Christian life. Over here are my "work" bricks—a bit dull and utilitarian, but very practical— and this rather grubby pile over here is my home and family. And this other pile with the stained-glass window insert—that's all my church activities.'

Even if we actually roll up our sleeves and begin the process of construction, we can be in such a hurry that we forget all about consulting God's plan. We're not too bothered about what exactly we are building so long as the walls go up quickly and look reasonably OK.

We may be tempted to cut corners when it comes to the materials we use, so the end result is something that looks really good on the outside, but actually isn't properly constructed at all.

It's easy to think, 'No one will notice that this bit of the building is weak—I know I have a problem with forgiving people who've hurt me, but I can lead people away from it so they won't notice. Or I can cover it up with a picture, or stand a decorative pot plant in front of it. No one's going to find out.' After all, no one's going to worry too much about what lies underneath, and a lick of spiritual gloss does wonders!

We have friends who commissioned an extension to house a farmhouse-style kitchen/dining-room. When it was finished it looked beautiful and everybody admired it—until the next heavy rainstorm.

Sadly, the builders had not used the type of brick the architect had specified. They had bought in a cheap lot of bricks instead, thinking they could cut costs.

The problem was that instead of keeping the rain out, the poor-quality porous bricks let the rain in. They looked identical to the real thing, but they didn't do what they were supposed to do.

Even more crucial than good-quality building materials is what holds it all together—the all-important foundation that gives strength, security and permanence to everything else that is built afterwards.

We might be tempted to discount the foundation. After all, you can't see it. Surely what goes on top is what really matters.

A house with no foundations can look really good above ground. It can have all the newest architectural features and a stunning designer interior—but if the foundations have been laid incorrectly or not at all, there will certainly be costly problems later on, and possibly even the total collapse of the building.

Laying a foundation is hard work. You will notice on a building site that this is what takes the time and makes the most mess—levelling the ground, digging down deep enough, removing what seems like mountains of earth and creating clouds of dust and grit.

Sometimes we make the mistake of skimping on the foundations that we choose to place within our lives, opting for temporary glitz rather than eternal values and truths.

The Bible tells us quite clearly that there is only one foundation on which a Christian can build: 'For no one can lay any foundation other than the one that has been laid; that foundation is Jesus Christ' (1 Corinthians 3:11).

This is what God requires, and however good or valuable other foundations might appear—our homes, our families, our work, our church activities, our relationships with others, good works—they are like sand in God's sight.

Don't be fooled—there is no substitute for the real thing. Jesus is the rock we build upon, a foundation guaranteed to withstand every storm that life has to offer.

PROVERBS WOMAN

✣

Proverbs woman

Have you ever felt tempted to skip over a certain passage in the Bible? You know the one I mean, the one at the very end of Proverbs 31 which lists the virtues of a truly remarkable woman.

Does reading about her character qualities make you only too aware of the weaknesses in your own? 'Proverbs woman? More like perfect woman,' you groan. 'How can I possibly ever measure up to such a high standard?'

Actually I get the feeling that Proverbs woman did not become the wonderful lady we read about overnight. If we look at the passage more closely there are some telling phrases.

The 'teaching of kindness... on her tongue' (v. 26) strongly suggests that a learning process has been involved. She has taught herself to say things that will upbuild and encourage others, rather than the clever put-downs and sarcastic remarks that so easily trip off our tongue in the daily routine.

We are also told that she 'girds herself with strength, and makes her arms strong' (v. 17). This reminds me of Ephesians 6:11–17, where we are instructed to put on the whole armour of God.

Proverbs woman makes a conscious decision each day to clothe herself in certain qualities, just as each day she would dress herself in the appropriate garments for her lifestyle.

Proverbs woman is:

- strong—not easily thrown by circumstances or situations.
- trustworthy—someone who can be relied on and will not betray confidences.
- willing—approaching jobs with a willing attitude rather than having to be coerced into doing things.
- disciplined—she has learnt how to prioritize and how to manage her time. She is a planner who would wholeheartedly endorse the saying, 'Those who fail to plan, plan to fail.'

- hardworking—not afraid of hard work. She is a woman who will get down to jobs rather than keep putting them off.
- openhearted—a giver, not just in her family and business, but to those in need. She is not too busy to find time for others.
- not a worrier—how many of us waste time and energy worrying about things over which we have no control and which may never happen? This woman is totally secure and can laugh at tomorrow.
- creative—involved in a variety of projects including gardening, dressmaking and cookery.
- dignified—someone who has a strong sense of self-worth. She knows who she is in God.
- kind—her success in business and in the home does not make her treat people badly. Her words reflect her caring attitude.
- supportive—there is no power struggle in her home, with husband and wife battling for dominance. She actively blesses her husband and children.
- Godfearing—above all, she is a woman who tries to live her life as God wants her to.
- happy—secure in herself, her family and her God, this woman radiates happiness.

The Proverbs woman could so easily have been different. Her success could have gone to her head and made her a bullying, dominant figure, hated and feared. But she chooses to be different.

But what makes her different, and can we learn from her example? Is it possible in this day and age to become a Proverbs woman or is she just too good to be true?

Perhaps we think, 'That's all very well, but this description was written in a different age with a different lifestyle. A woman like that had a large household to run and plenty of servants to help her do it. What can she possibly have to say to a modern woman like me?'

Or perhaps we feel overawed by this woman. After all, she seems to combine the rôles of successful businesswoman, excellent wife, superb household manager and wise mother with comparative ease. Many of us struggle to find our feet in just one of these areas! Do we think despairingly, 'I'd love to be like her, but Lord, I haven't got a hope!'

What is her secret? How did she become the woman that we read about? Did she attend a course on 'How to Combine Housewifery with a Flourishing Business' or was she just blessed with an unusually successful blend of character qualities?

While her list of achievements is impressive, this is not what really marks out the woman of Proverbs. The simple key to becoming an effective Proverbs woman is found close to the end of the passage.

Interestingly, we never find out whether the Proverbs woman is beautiful or not (although I am sure she has an inner beauty of the spirit). The most precious quality she possesses is not her looks, her financial expertise, her thriftiness or her homemaking skills but the fact that she fears the Lord (v. 30). The Bible tells us:

- 'The fear of the Lord is the beginning of wisdom' (Proverbs 9:10).
- 'The fear of the Lord prolongs life' (Proverbs 10:27).
- 'In the fear of the Lord one has strong confidence' (Proverbs 14:26).
- 'The fear of the Lord is a fountain of life' (Proverbs 14:27).

This is the bedrock of the Proverbs woman's life—the fear of the Lord. It is because she fears him that she has become the woman she is.

We may not be able to do half the things at which the Proverbs woman excels, but this is one area in which we can all be like her—in cultivating a fear of the Lord and bringing every aspect of our day to him.

As we do so, we may notice a surprising thing happening. We may find ourselves learning strength and kindness, wisdom and self-control —in fact, the fruits of the spirit that we find so plainly exhibited in the life of the woman in Proverbs 31.

However, God doesn't want us to be carbon copies of that woman. While the woman in Proverbs is in many ways a pattern of Christian womanhood and there is much that we can learn from her, God doesn't want us slavishly to follow her routines. Getting up at the crack of dawn to buy food or investing in a plot of land will not make us a Proverbs woman.

God wants you to be the woman he has created you to be—the Proverbs woman in your street, in your business, waiting at the school gate, in the supermarket queue, in the waiting-room at the doctor's or dentist's surgery.

Have you ever worn one of those name badges to identify yourself at a meeting? Well, God has one of those for you. It reads 'Proverbs Woman ——.' Put your name in the gap: as a woman who fears God, it belongs there!

❖

Driving lesson

I well remember the first time I took my son out for a practice drive when he was beginning driving lessons. Before I stepped into the car I resolved that whatever happened I would remain calm, absolutely calm. Easier said than done—rarely have I felt such nail-biting tension!

From the time the car door shuts on the pair of you, it seems that every sense is heightened. 'Put your seatbelt on,' you say. He's even forgotten that!

The key turns and even though you're in a level car park, as far away from all the other cars as possible, your palms feel clammy and your heart is in your mouth.

The car kangaroos forward with your son muttering in exasperation. The accelerator revs, making the old banger you've bought (there's no way your husband will let him loose in his car!) sound like a Ferrari. 'Not so hard,' you plead.

He moves off slowly and you crane your neck to impossible angles looking out for potential hazards—the old lady with her shopping, that car nosing out from the left.

Half an hour later the practice drive is over. He is pleased with himself. Inwardly you are shaking like a leaf. 'Well done,' you say through clenched teeth.

'Can we go out on the proper road next time?'

You suppress a shudder. 'I don't think you're quite ready yet.'

'Aw, Mum!'

Things get better slowly but surely. After a few more weeks the car is no longer jerking and he doesn't keep making that horrific crunching noise as he fails to engage the gears correctly yet again.

He learns to move off smoothly at traffic lights and park close to the kerb instead of several feet away. He chooses the right lane at roundabouts and can even execute near-perfect reverse parking—something you've never totally mastered!

At first you had to constantly remind him what to do next.

'Check your mirror before moving out.'

'Signal in plenty of time.'

'You're driving too fast. This is a 30mph zone!'

However, as he masters each new skill, and then moves on to the next, you are able to sit back in your seat and, if not quite relax, at least have enough confidence in the level he has reached to feel that he should be able to cope with most of the situations he encounters.

How different from the early days! Then there would be times when he'd panic and want to opt out. Perhaps the car would stall at a busy junction or he'd get stuck in the middle of a tricky three-point turn in a narrow road.

At those times he'd feel despairingly that he would never get the hang of it, and it would be your job to comfort and encourage him, take the keys, slide over into the driving seat and get him out of the sticky situation in which he found himself.

It's second nature to our mothering instincts, isn't it—to rescue our kids when they are in trouble? Being a mother is hard. We so want to protect and shelter our children.

When they are babies they rely on us for everything, and as they grow up we seek to instil in them the character and values of a Christian family which are so important to us.

In effect, at that point we are in the driving seat, choosing the direction in which they will go, selecting the most appropriate gear and speed. As young children they have no say at all.

As they grow older, things change. They want to learn driving skills for themselves and at times may even try to take over the steering wheel before they are mature enough to do so.

Through the years, there will be many times when we slip the car into a different gear for them or put a hand on the steering wheel to prevent them taking a bend too fast. And, of course, we are always there to offer verbal encouragement and advice from the driving manual—to remind them what the principles of good driving are and to encourage them to put them into practice.

However, just as with driving lessons, as time goes on there must be a releasing of the young driver. By the time he or she comes to take the test, the skills you have instilled in your child with so much patience will, you hope, be second nature.

You hope that your teaching has given them an ability to drive well and safely and to respect other road users. You have taught them all you know as well as you can but the day comes when you are no longer needed to oversee your child's driving.

Waving a piece of paper, they tell you ecstatically that they have passed the test. From now on they can take the car out on their own without someone constantly at their side, ready to correct their faults and point out potential dangers.

Those first few drives when they go off on their own are scary. As a mother, you can imagine so many different scenarios.

'What if she drives too fast and ends up in a ditch?'

'Will he remember to switch his lights on when it gets dark?'

'Will she forget to take the keys out of the engine and lock herself out of the car?'

'What if he crashes?'

Do we feel tempted to hang on to our children, to be a backseat driver constantly trying to control their driving skills? Or can we hand over the keys willingly in spite of the sense of loss, knowing that our young ones are ready to spread their wings and fly solo?

Can we take our hands off, step back, and wish them 'God Speed' as they take to life's highway on their own account?

Be·ers and doers

Jesus is coming to the home of Mary and Martha.

For Mary, this means preparing herself to come into her Lord's presence. She waits eagerly for him, determined to spend as much time as she possibly can at his side. She doesn't want to miss a single word he says. From the moment he arrives, she wants to be with him in the same room, to study his beloved face, to listen to his wisdom. Nothing will distract her from that.

Poor Martha. For her, a visitor—and such a visitor—means hours of endless preparation. No doubt she was up at dawn, scrubbing and scouring to make her house fit to receive him.

Then there was the trip to the market, choosing the freshest and choicest ingredients, and now comes the food preparation, the chopping of herbs and grinding of pungent spices. She is determined that this will be a meal fit for a king. After all, she believes that this is the Messiah. Everything must be perfect.

If only Mary would help more. But no, she spends half the time watching out for him, and then, as soon as he comes, makes his arrival the excuse to drop everything. Trust her to leave everything to Martha. Does she think the work gets done by itself?

Perhaps Martha feels an ache in her heart as she slaves over the kitchen stove. How she would love to be in there with him too. But she can't. Luke 10:40 tells us that she was 'distracted by her many tasks'. Martha's got far too much to do to spend time listening to her beloved Lord.

Meanwhile, Mary is sitting right at Jesus' feet, totally focused on him and what he is saying. She doesn't feel pressure to get on with life's business. She has separated the important from the unimportant.

She wants to hear from God—to feast on the living word, not on an elaborately prepared banquet. She is listening with everything that is within her, not just with her ears but with her heart.

In the kitchen, hot and flustered, Martha can hear the others laughing. They sound so happy. Does no one care that she is out here all alone, soldiering on, bearing the burden? Where is Mary? Why should she just sit there doing nothing, listening to Jesus?

I feel a lot of sympathy for Martha. She is like so many of us who take on more than we can easily cope with, who reach saturation point, swamped by too many tasks in our lives.

Sometimes we need to take a long, hard look at our lifestyle. Are we rushing around all the time, permanently trying to catch up with ourselves and feeling as though we're stuck on a treadmill, running harder and harder but never actually getting anywhere?

Have we lost sight of what should be most important to us—our relationship with the living God buried beneath our busy agendas?

I think that Martha probably knew she had made the wrong choice and that with all her heart and soul she longed to be in there with Mary. She must have wondered why on earth she had given herself so much to do, why she had driven herself to the point of exhaustion so that she was too tired, too bogged down in what she was doing, too angry with Mary, to spend precious time with Jesus.

As is often the case when we've got ourselves into a fix, we look around for something or someone to blame, and Martha found the ideal candidate: Mary, her sister the dreamer, her sister who would sit idly by while she, Martha, worked her fingers to the bone.

Of course, if Mary had helped more, Martha would have been able to sit at Jesus' feet too—to laugh with him, listen to him, learn from him.

Martha's anger and tiredness spills out in a sense of injustice and grievance against her sister who, she sees with annoyance, is not bone tired but refreshed, renewed, inspired.

She wants Jesus to tell her off, to say to Mary, 'Look how Martha has worn herself out in my service. Look at all she's done for me. Look how tired she is. *She* can't sit at my feet, because she is still working.'

Mary can't understand Martha either. How can Martha shut herself away in the kitchen when Jesus is right here? Why doesn't she just drop what she's doing? What could be more important than to spend time with Jesus?

Jesus looks into Martha's heart and sees her confusion, the pressures of her life constricting her with so many deadlines to be met, cutting her off from the source of peace that she so much needs and longs for. Her life is so filled with activity that the one thing she wants more than anything else is squeezed out:

- time to be with him
- time just to sit at his feet
- time not to do but to be—with him

Gently he reminds her that she has allowed herself to be distracted from the one thing that really matters—her love relationship with him.

As we rush round from task to task, our heads throbbing, our feet aching as we strive to achieve and do, have we realized that something is missing from our lives? Can we hear the laughter coming from another room that we long to enter?

Jesus said to the care-laden Martha, 'There is need of only one thing…' (Luke 10:42).

Let's lay aside the tasks that bow us down with their weight, many of them self-inflicted, and let's open the door and go in to join Mary.

What she is doing is not nothing.

What she is doing is everything.

Sitting at Jesus' feet, she finds everything that her heart, her soul and her mind need—streams of water in the desert, the glorious fountain of life.

Learn to be a Mary, someone who is content to just 'be' in the presence of Jesus and, like her, find rest for your soul.

❖

Perfect pastry

Have you got a cookbook that is your particular favourite? If you use it a lot, the likelihood is that it has a somewhat battered appearance. Perhaps the pages are a bit dog-eared. There may even be a few stains where ingredients have splashed on to its pages.

Actually this is the sign of a good cookbook. Only one that is hardly ever open will be in pristine condition. The scruffy one is the one that you use all the time, the one that consistently gives good results. You know that you can trust the recipes in this particular book and that if you follow the instructions the result will be an appetizing meal to serve up to the family at dinnertime.

Have you ever thought about the recipes in a cookery book? A recipe is just a listing of ingredients, but as you follow the directions and blend them all together, what you end up with is something quite different from all those individual substances.

Just looking at the ingredients written down, it is hard to believe that the finished result can be so delicious. Flour, milk and butter don't amount to much on their own, but combine them with cheese or freshly chopped parsley and you have a tasty, mouth-watering sauce.

Cookery skills develop with experience and some are harder than others. You may be a dab hand at trifles but your sponges never rise properly, or perhaps you have never quite got the hang of good pancake batter.

I have always been told that one way to judge a person's culinary skills is to sample their pastry, that this is the acid test of a good cook. When I got married, my pastry-making skills were non-existent, and I wasn't sure if I even wanted to try. I had heard so many things about pastry-making. It sounded a hugely complicated business.

'You need a light touch for pastry.'

'Cool hands produce the best result.'

Everybody I spoke to seemed to have their own idea about how to produce the best results. Should I use lard, butter or margarine, or a combination; cold water or milk to mix; plain flour or wholemeal flour? No wonder I felt confused.

I had vivid memories of trying to 'make pastry' as a child and of the heavy, grey, speckled lump I ended up with. Pastry-making seemed to be one of those awkward skills that were difficult to get right, and I suspected that any attempts I made would fall far short of edibility. It would be much safer and easier to stick to frozen pastry from the local supermarket.

Occasionally I would have yet another try. In my mind would be an image of a beautiful golden-brown pie, artistically decorated with leaves and sprigs, but somehow in those early days, and in spite of my best efforts, success eluded me.

However carefully I followed the recipe, the pastry was never quite right—undercooked, overcooked, leaden or dust-dry. Why couldn't I get the hang of it? It certainly was an uphill struggle.

For many of us, there are certain aspects of our character that let us down and we find it hard to deal with the problem. Our initial attempts at following God's recipes for the Christian life are not very successful and leave us feeling despondent and discouraged.

Why do we have such problems controlling our temper? Where is the inner peace that God promises us?

We sometimes feel we've put our pie dish, with its carefully combined ingredients, into the oven in good faith, expecting to produce a delicious and nourishing meal that will bless those around us; yet the minute our back is turned, the whole lot disintegrates into a charred mess that we then have to spend time and energy clearing up.

Why is it so difficult to produce Christian character in our lives? We want to be the aroma of Christ, not the pungent, acrid smell of yet another burnt offering.

Wouldn't it be lovely if there was some sort of instantaneous, failsafe recipe for Christian character?

Take 125g compassion, 100g joy and 50g patience. Add a teaspoon of self-control and two cloves of goodness. Mix with the oil of peace, place in oven on Gas Mark 4 for 40 minutes until well risen. Leave for five minutes and then turn out on to a cooling rack. Fill with fresh praise.

Unfortunately it's not that simple. Christian character, like culinary skill, is not something that happens overnight. It is something we need to work at and perfect.

Creating a dish from scratch, even when following a recipe, is not as easy as it seems, especially if you're a relative beginner. It takes plenty of practice to discover how to blend a smooth, creamy white sauce, bake a light and delicious sponge or produce golden pastry that flakes at the touch of a fork.

In the same way, although all the instructions are there for us in the Bible, and there is a recipe for every situation in which we may ever find ourselves, it takes time to build up the skills we need to produce the required effect:

- to mix judgment with love, producing compassion
- to sift what is set before us in the light of God's word
- to combine the complementary ingredients of faith and works

As children, we tend to overhandle pastry, pushing and pulling it about so much in an attempt to get it right that we end up with a greyish lump. It is only as we come to understand exactly what the recipe requires and how to go about it that our cooking techniques improve, enabling us to tackle with relative ease the things that used to cause us such problems.

The recipe has always been the same but we have become familiar with the skills necessary to produce it. We now know how to rub the fat into the flour, how much liquid to incorporate and that a period of rest enables the pastry to be rolled out smoothly.

In fact, we don't even need to have the book open in front of us every time we make pastry. We have followed the recipe so often that we know exactly what to do and what quantities to use. We know precisely how much liquid we must add to make the pastry the right consistency for that 'melt-in-the-mouth' quality.

We do it almost without thinking, because the skills we've learned so painstakingly over months and years have become second nature to us.

Those time-consuming and difficult dishes that used to make us weep with frustration as we failed again and again to get it right—the

'Not Criticizing your Neighbour Gateau', the 'Fricassée of Humility with tender sprigs of fresh Kindness and par-boiled Steadfastness' and the 'Matured Casserole of jointed Wisdom with a soupçon of Servanthood seasoned with Grace'—are finally within our grasp.

Sometimes, disappointingly, we find that a recipe in a cookery book is inaccurate and fails to live up to the promising illustration on the page. The timing is obviously wrong, or perhaps the word 'tablespoon' has replaced 'teaspoon' as a measure, with disastrous effects.

The Bible is not like that. It will not let us down as we follow its directions carefully in order to blend and combine the ingredients that make up the character of a godly woman. These are the original and best, tried and tested recipes with guaranteed results. All we have to do is follow them.

❖

Guess who's coming to dinner?

Normally when we give an invitation to dinner we know exactly who to expect on the night. We've probably had at least a few days to think about menus, to do the shopping and get the ingredients we need. Perhaps if we're really well organized we've even prepared the pudding the night before so that we're not rushing around in a last-minute panic.

The table is laid and we're ready to present a smiling face to our guests. Relaxing music plays in the background and there's no hint of the frantic activity of just ten minutes ago, when we were dashing from saucepan to saucepan, turning the heat up under one to make sure the contents got cooked in time, while carefully stirring the sauce in another to stop it turning into a congealed mush.

It's hard enough to cope when we know what's happening in advance, but what happens when we're totally unprepared and someone just turns up unexpectedly?

I wonder how Sarah felt when Abraham came into the tent by the oaks of Mamre and asked her to bake some cakes quickly for three unexpected guests (Genesis 18:6).

The guests hadn't arrived at a convenient time. It was the very hottest part of the day. I am sure the last thing Sarah wanted to do was to bake cakes. How much nicer just to relax in the shade.

It must have been tempting not to bother very much. Surely the strangers ought to be content with a cold drink? After all, these people weren't friends or family. Why put yourself out for someone you don't even know?

However, Abraham and Sarah, in accordance with their culture's tradition of hospitality, ignored the inconvenience to themselves and did everything they could to make their guests welcome. Water was brought so that the strangers could bathe their feet, and then they were encouraged to rest while Abraham and Sarah busied themselves in preparing food.

They didn't just grab a few odds and ends—yesterday's slightly stale bread and the leftover stew from the previous evening. Sarah got out the choice flour, not just the everyday variety, and kneaded it to make fine cakes while Abraham selected a young calf to provide tender, succulent meat for the main course.

You can sense that Abraham and Sarah felt a real joy in preparing the meal for their visitors. They didn't drag their heels as they got the ingredients together. You don't get the impression that either of them thought, 'Oh, I wish those men hadn't turned up today. I'll get them some food, but don't expect me to put myself out in the process.'

On the contrary, there is an urgency about everything they do, an eagerness to serve their guests, to put their own comfort second as they hastily concoct a meal from the finest ingredients they have available—a sense that only the best will do.

I wonder how we would feel if we were asked to feed three complete strangers at a moment's notice. What emotions would we experience —panic, resentment, maybe even anger?

Many of us would find it difficult to be like Abraham and Sarah, coping so graciously and with such a serving attitude. Very often, security for us lies in our own carefully controlled hospitality rout-ines. We tend to invite only those people we get along with, and that usually means people who are similar to us. We feel threatened by anything else.

I wonder how we would feel if Zacchaeus the unpopular tax collector turned up for supper (Luke 19:7), or we found ourselves sharing a fondue with Simon the leper (Matthew 26:6). What would happen if a well-known local prostitute turned up in our dining-room? Would we welcome her or would our immediate reaction be, 'What will the neighbours think?'

Hospitality is one of the most precious ministries for Christians. If Christians don't invite those who lack acceptance into their homes, who else is going to do it?

Jesus ate with all sorts of people:

- noisy, exuberant children
- men from every level of society—educated, uneducated, rich, poor

- women, at that time considered by many to be second-class citizens
- influential religious leaders
- those who opposed him
- those who were sick in body or spirit
- those who were shunned by everybody else

Offering hospitality is far more than just eating food together. It has nothing to do with how well the table is set or whether the meal is of cordon bleu standard.

True hospitality says to the other person, 'I want to share a part of my life with you. I want to open myself up, to make myself vulnerable, and in the process get to know you better.'

I don't think it's an accident that verse 9 in 1 Peter 4, 'Be hospitable to one another without complaining', is sandwiched between verse 8 which encourages us to 'maintain constant love for one another' and verse 10 which tells us to 'serve one another'. To me that sums up the very essence of hospitality—love and serving.

When Abraham and Sarah set the meal in front of their unexpected guests, I am sure they had no thought of getting anything in return, but actually there was fruit from their sacrificial hospitality to three strangers. To their surprise and delight, they found that God himself was present at the meal.

It's the same when we take the step of willingly opening our hearts and our homes in reaching out to others. God turns up. As we share meals and our hearts with others, there is an extra guest at the table, the real host who welcomes each one of us in his name.

Sitting at the table in his presence, the weary are refreshed, the wounded are healed, the lonely find a friend, those who mourn find new joy and those who are lost find salvation.

'For I was hungry and you gave me food, I was thirsty and you gave me something to drink, I was a stranger and you welcomed me' (Matthew 25:35).

❖

Traffic jam

It's supposed to be a motorway with a 70mph limit, the quickest route from A to B, but right now a pedal cyclist could easily overtake you. Cars inch forward nose to tail, a long, winding, metallic caterpillar as far as the eye can see, and at this point you really wish you'd stuck to the scenic A roads.

Motorways—a modern marvel when things go right, a modern instrument of torture when things go wrong. Trapped in your small metal box, the children beginning to squabble in the back, you face the perennial puzzle of whether to stick it out and hope the situation improves, or leave the motorway at the next junction.

What do we do when traffic isn't moving and the queues stretch for miles? It's funny how traffic jams often bring out our worst qualities.

Do we notice that the traffic in the other lane seems to be moving faster and sneak into that one, only to find that the lane we were originally in suddenly frees up and we're left even further behind?

Do we cut up other motorists—seeing a gap and swiftly pulling into it, regardless of the consequences? Behind us there is a frantic slamming-on of brakes and several near-accidents, but what do we care? Opportunities for progress need to be seized boldly. At last we're getting somewhere!

Do we get just as frustrated when we cannot understand why God is delaying? To us the course of action is so obvious.

'Lord, heal me.'

'Lord, help my finances.'

'Lord, give me that new job.'

'Lord, save my daughter/son.'

When God does not respond as we expect, we can grow confused. 'If God loves me then surely he would do this, so maybe he doesn't love me after all.'

From there it's often a short step to anger and bitterness. 'Well, if God is like that, I don't want to know him any more.'

For some of us, traffic jams make us doubt the whole road system. Instead of seeing the jam as one annoying facet of travelling on the road, we find fault with the whole route network.

We get so focused on the fact that we are stuck, we forget that the traffic jam is just an obstacle on the way to our final destination. Whether we are at a standstill or travelling at full speed, we are still on the motorway.

Time spent in traffic queues is not pleasant. It seems like wasted time, sitting there tapping your fingers on the wheel and waiting for the traffic to move on. It is easy to lose your temper—perhaps with other people in the car, or maybe with other motorists.

When prayers aren't answered we become impatient with well-meaning people who offer help and advice. 'What does she know? She's never been in this situation. It's easy for her to talk!'

Traffic jams do not seem to serve a useful purpose from the perspective of the stationary driver, but they're something that all motorists have to face at some point. Sometimes they are just minor hiccups, short delays that barely affect us, but sometimes they involve lengthy periods of waiting when we are unable to move forward at all.

Sometimes we get into traffic jams because we have not bothered to check out the route in advance. If we had listened to the traffic news before travelling, we would have known that there were potential hazards along this particular route, and avoided it.

Or perhaps we did hear the forecast but decided to ignore it and take the route anyway. Perhaps we persuaded ourselves that the reports were exaggerated or that the traffic problems would have disappeared by the time we reached that stretch of road.

The Bible gives us ample warning about possible dangers that may block our progress as Christians. If we still choose to run those risks, we should not be surprised if we find ourselves ensnared in a traffic jam, unable to extricate ourselves until we have slowly and painfully worked our way through the obstacles.

However, sometimes we get stuck through no fault of our own. Perhaps there has been an unforeseen accident that stops us in our tracks—tragic events such as serious illness, job loss, marital break-down, or a death. All these things can make it difficult for us to continue the journey, slowing us down or even stopping us altogether for a while.

Traffic jams make us feel inadequate. We sit behind the wheel but we can't use it. We know where we should be going but we can't get there.

Our emotions range from impatience to frustration, from bitterness to anger. We're stuck—not going anywhere. And sometimes, in spiritual terms, we're tempted to conclude that because we can't move on, the whole drive has been a waste of time. What point is there in continuing?

If someone abandoned their journey just because of a traffic jam, we would think, 'How silly! Why don't they just sit it out? They'll get moving eventually.'

In spiritual terms we need to remember that God knows exactly where we are at any particular time on the road, and that he watches tenderly over our progress. Whether we are in a traffic jam through our own fault or because of circumstances beyond our control, he wants us to get going again.

Each traffic jam we encounter is different. God may require us to sit this particular traffic jam out to the bitter end with his help: 'Wait for the Lord; be strong, and let your heart take courage; wait for the Lord!' (Psalm 27:14).

At other times he may lead us into quiet side roads for a while before we rejoin the busy main thoroughfare at a point further on. Or he may even arrange for us to draw aside into a service station for refreshment and to replenish dwindling fuel supplies.

One thing is certain. There is no obstacle on the road so great that we cannot overcome it with his help. No longer at a frustrating standstill, the hedgerows flash by. We press on, knowing that our destination lies ahead at the end of the road.

✤

Simon says

Have you ever noticed how important it is for teenagers to have a group identity? How they all buy the latest hi-tech gizmo, listen fanatically to CDs of the band that is currently flavour of the month, and wear similar clothes?

Has it ever puzzled you that when choosing between two virtually identical pairs of jeans, one is 'in' and the other is 'out' simply because the first sports a trendy logo and the second does not?

As adults we may think we're above such things, but are we? Perhaps it is not so obvious but in subtle ways we fall victim to the same pressures to conform.

Think about it for a moment. Do we behave in the same way when we're with Christians as when we're with those who are not believers? Are there certain subjects that we don't discuss because we don't want to be the odd one out, to stand out from the crowd?

Group identity is a real pressure—the need to be accepted, to blend in, even if it means compromising our beliefs. It reminds me of the children's game 'Simon Says', where you have to follow the leader exactly, and if you get it wrong you're out.

Are we following a sort of 'Simon Says' policy in our lives?

Society says, 'Don't say that something is immoral or wrong. It could make you unpopular.'

Society says, 'Don't worry about inner values; materialism is what counts.'

Society says, 'Moan about your boss as much as you like. Everybody else does.'

We might think that at least within the church we are safe from such double standards, but, sadly, spiritual 'Simon Says' is just as popular as the more materialistic version outside. Are we doing things because we honestly feel from our hearts that this is what God wants us to do, or are we simply following the crowd without really thinking it through?

Has participation in the Sunday service become something so familiar that we're almost on automatic pilot? Are we singing the hymns and choruses without really paying any attention to the words? Are we just making a pleasant sound, or are we engaged in praising God with the whole of our being?

What about praying? Has it become just a form of words that we follow, or do we actually mean what we say?

These are tough questions that stop us in our tracks, but we do need to evaluate where we are in our Christian lives. We can seem as if we've 'got it together' as Christians, at least on the surface, but is our heart in what we are doing or are we just going through the motions?

Remember the story of Sapphira and her husband Ananias (Acts 5:1–11). It's probably one that we prefer to forget. This couple wanted people to think they were like Barnabas, sacrificially giving the whole purchase price of their land to the church.

What they were really doing, however, was mimicking the behaviour of others. It wasn't real for them. Simon says: 'Do what everyone else is doing, not because you want to do it in your heart, but for the sake of appearances.'

We need to be totally honest with ourselves. Why are we running the Sunday school, singing in the choir or music group, or leading a home group? Is it because that's what people do when they've reached a certain level in our church, or do we passionately believe that we're doing it for God?

There are far too many people even in our churches who simply copy others instead of being true to themselves and to what God has called them to be.

Jesus himself broke all the traditional patterns for a religious leader in his day. He didn't fast—he enjoyed eating and drinking. He didn't confine himself to mixing with other spiritual leaders. He was out there rubbing shoulders with the most unsuitable people—ill-educated, rough fishermen, prostitutes and shady business dealers.

Jesus certainly didn't follow the crowd. He was far more concerned with pleasing God than popular opinion.

I like J.B. Phillips' translation of Romans 12:2: 'Do not let the world around you squeeze you into its own mould.' How do we behave in everyday life? Are we afraid to do what we should do because it means we must move out from the safety of the group? Do we allow the herd instinct to stop us saying what we really think, being who we really are?

Paul writes tellingly in Galatians 1:10, 'Am I now seeking human approval, or God's approval? Or am I trying to please people? If I were still pleasing people, I would not be a servant of Christ.'

They're strong words, but true. If we're seriously going to follow Christ, there will be times when what we say and how we behave will cut across popular trends.

Christians are meant to be different. We are meant to be lights, to shine out, not to blend in. Simon says—or Jesus says? The choice is yours.

LEEKS AND CUCUMBERS

⁘

Leeks and cucumbers

You can imagine the temptation for the Israelites. They're going to God's promised land, or so they've been told. It's a land flowing with milk and honey by all accounts, but where on earth is it? They've been stuck in this desert for ages and they're fed up with looking at the monotonous scenery, just planting one foot in front of the other, eating the same old food.

Manna was all very well at first, but remember what it was like back in Egypt? Those firm, green-skinned cucumbers, the luscious figs and juicy grapes fresh from the vine. Delicious! (Numbers 11:5–6).

It was not in the thick of battle that the niggling dissatisfactions started—there was far too much to think about then. But as the tedium of the journey set in, they began to wonder what they were doing there and why they ever left Egypt in the first place.

When they began the journey, everything was new and exciting. They had the sense of starting a new life, clearly knowing that God was with them. But as one day succeeded another and the Israelites never seemed to get any nearer to what God had promised, they couldn't help looking back with regret.

It was true there were all those bricks to make, but then there were the pomegranates and savoury-tasting leeks as compensation. Perhaps Egypt wasn't really so bad after all.

'Remember the luxuries back there? It almost doesn't bear thinking about—all those delicacies to choose from, and a roof to sleep beneath each night. Have I really made the right choice? Why don't I turn back? At least I knew where I was in Egypt.'

It's easy for us to condemn the Israelites. 'How could they be like that?' we cry. 'God brought them out of slavery in the land of Egypt and here they are pining for leeks and cucumbers!'

Actually it's when the Christian life is sheer hard plodding that most of us feel the lure of the old 'Egypt', the pressure to give up trudging along and turn back to where we were before.

The Israelites suffered from a sort of spiritual tunnel vision. Every time they were in a tight situation, their instinct was to run away, to return to the old security of their slavery, rather than wait and see what God would do.

Talk about selective memories! They could have looked back on what had happened since Moses first challenged Pharaoh and seen how God had delivered them over and over again.

- When the Israelites cried out to God to free them from slavery in Egypt, God sent a series of plagues until Pharaoh released them (Exodus 7:20—12:32).
- When the Egyptians pursued them, God opened a path to safety through the Red Sea (Exodus 14:5–29).
- When the water was bitter at Marah, God sweetened it (Exodus 15:22–25).
- When they were hungry, God fed them with bread from heaven (Exodus 16:14–35).
- When they were thirsty, God provided them with water from the rock (Exodus 17:3–6).

The Israelites had seen God's miraculous protection and provision for them, yet there was still something inside them that cried, 'Why did we ever leave Egypt?'

We all have our own personal Egypt, that place which is so familiar to us and where it would be so easy to settle back once more, even though we know that it's not what God wants for us. What we have already known, our own personal comfort zone, can stop us moving on with God.

We're not sure we really want to go any further. After all, who knows what Canaan will be like? It might turn out to be overrated and a huge disappointment.

Egypt is different. Back there, life was easier—there weren't all these challenges. The trouble is, we like the taste of leeks and cucumbers. We've grown up with it and it's what we're used to. Bread of heaven? Well, I'm not sure—it's rather an acquired taste, isn't it? And Canaan? It's a long, long way from here.

We have two choices. We can get stuck in our past with an 'Egypt' mentality, continually looking back and complaining about how much better things were before, forgetting that actually it was the place where we were enslaved. Or we can adopt a 'Canaan' mentality, recognizing what God has already done in our lives and moving boldly out into unknown territory with him at our side.

The Israelites could have got to Canaan years before, but because they were trapped in an Egypt mentality they ended up going round and round in circles.

Metaphorically speaking, they had not left their baggage behind—those thoughts and feelings and yearnings that should have remained in Egypt. Everywhere they went they dragged the past along, allowing it to weigh them down and continually pull them in the wrong direction.

If they'd been able to leave those suitcases labelled 'Egypt' behind, how much freer they would have been—able to follow God with a light step and heart, without unnecessary encumbrances.

What luggage are you carrying as you set out on your exciting journey with God? Is it labelled 'Canaan' and packed with things that will help you to go forward, or are you also weighed down by luggage labelled 'Egypt', containing all those things that you can't quite manage to let go?

It takes a lot of courage to leave all the stuff from Egypt behind, but it is the only way to enter God's promised land. God wants us to take only what belongs to Canaan.

We may feel vulnerable as we walk away from the old routines, the old habits and the old companions. We may even feel afraid as we walk in a direction that is totally new to us, somewhere we have never been before. But we are not alone.

Just as the Israelites had the pillar of cloud to guide them through the daytime and the pillar of fire at night, we too can experience God's guiding hand. 'The Lord has taken you and brought you out of the iron-smelter, out of Egypt, to become a people of his very own possession' (Deuteronomy 4:20)—no longer slaves, but free.

Potter and clay

Have you ever tried to make a pot? I have. As I watched the potter at work, I thought it looked so easy. Operating the wheel, keeping the clay moist, shaping it into the required form—everything he did was performed smoothly and without haste or confusion. Coaxing the dull-looking lump of clay with his fingers, the potter took only minutes to transform it magically into an elegant vase.

When it was my turn, I found that in my hands the obedient clay behaved totally differently, seeming to possess a will of its own and obstinately refusing to do anything I wanted.

Just getting the clay centred on the wheel caused me problems. I couldn't judge the speed correctly, and each time the ball of clay landed off-centre in spite of my best efforts.

After two or three unsuccessful and increasingly frustrated attempts, the potter took pity and did it for me, but my problems were far from over. In fact, they were only just beginning.

The clay slipped and slid beneath my hands like a slippery eel. When I tried to copy the potter and draw the sides up smoothly into a vaguely vase-like shape, they wobbled dangerously and threatened to collapse. Frantically I tried to save the bulging left-hand wall, but my attempts just made things even worse. This wasn't a pot—it was a lopsided blancmange. Help!

What a relief when the potter positioned his skilful hands along-side mine. 'Like this,' he said. Guided by him, the ballooning curves regained symmetry. The clay knew who was in control now and behaved impeccably, rising smoothly and giving no further trouble.

The Bible describes God as a master potter and us as the clay in several passages including Isaiah 29:16 and 45:9.

Making a pot is a more complicated process than we might realize. First there is the material, the basic clay from which the pot will be formed. Clay cannot be used just as it is. First, it goes through a series of processes to make it more malleable, so that it can be easily shaped and moulded by the potter's hands. Clay that is too stiff is no good for making pots.

In us, 'stiffness' can be caused by many things—a resistance to God, an unwillingness to be used by him, a hardness because of things that have hurt or offended us.

Human potters will take dry clay and fit it for use by adding water until the right consistency is reached. We may feel dried out and brittle, but if we allow the Holy Spirit to refresh us, we too will become pliable once again, ready for the Master to use.

The next stage is to bang the clay with the palm of the hand, to remove air pockets and also so that any impurities that shouldn't be there, such as stones or pieces of grass, can be removed.

If the clay is not prepared thoroughly in this way, cracks may appear later because of hidden deficiencies. Things that taint the clay prevent it from being the quality needed to make a good pot.

In us, imperfections like envy, irritability, or a tendency to be quarrelsome will also need to come under the loving discipline of the Potter's hand. Removing these flaws may be a painful process but the resulting clay will be of a much higher quality and easier to work with.

An important quality in clay is what potters call 'plasticity'—the ability to be readily moulded into whatever shape the potter requires. The more malleable the clay, the more easily the potter will be able to fashion it into a thing of beauty.

Being willing to be moulded by the Maker's hand is not an easy quality to develop when our society today emphasizes the importance of self-reliance, standing on your own two feet, thinking for yourself. We can obstruct what God wants to do in our lives or we can willingly submit and allow hm to do his perfect work.

When it is time to begin forming the pot, it is essential that the clay is centred correctly on the wheel. Clay that is off-centre will distort and even collapse.

We also need to be centred on God or we will find greater and greater imbalance in our lives. Our 'pot' will wobble and show a tendency to disintegrate under pressure.

Once the clay is successfully centred, the potter doesn't walk off and leave it. He doesn't say, 'Get on with it. Become a pot!' There is an intimacy between the potter and the pot. He is involved at every stage of its creation, constantly dampening the clay to keep it supple and workable, and applying just enough pressure for a graceful shape to be formed. The pot comes into being through the constant touch of his hands.

It is the same with us: whatever pressures we may be experiencing and however much we feel in danger of collapsing, God's hands hold us safe. He patiently and lovingly corrects our tendency to warp and distort, refashioning us and creating a beautiful vessel as we allow him to shape us through our circumstances.

If you visit a pottery, you will see that no two handmade pots are exactly alike, but you can often recognize that they are made by the same person because they carry certain elements of that potter's style, perhaps in the type of glaze used or in the decoration.

In the same way, the Potter who takes our clay and moulds it imparts his own unique signature to the pots that he has made.

Pots can have a variety of uses. One might be designed as a candle holder, another to contain a glossy-leaved houseplant, yet another to serve as a beautiful ornament for the mantelpiece.

We too are created for a purpose—to be filled with the essence of Jesus. In 2 Corinthians 4:7 it talks of 'treasure in clay jars'.

A clay pot is made of the humblest of materials and is nothing much to look at, but if it bears the imprint of the Master Potter's touch and contains the 'treasure' of a life yielded and moulded to his purposes, it is transformed into a vessel fit for the King of kings.

Forbidden fruit

We had a rule when our children were little that they weren't allowed to touch the flip-top rubbish bin in the kitchen. From our point of view, the bin contained things like leftover scraps of food that we did not want little fingers to come into contact with, because they might harbour germs.

However, this excellent reasoning meant nothing to our children. As far as they were concerned, the bin was an attractive piece of play equipment that drew them like a magnet.

The lid swung enticingly to and fro when pressed by a finger, and it was exciting to post pieces of puzzle and farm animals through the opening of this nice, brightly coloured plastic box and watch them disappear.

Our youngest son was particularly fascinated and many times would sidle closer and closer to the bin, a cherubic smile on his face but with his little hand outstretched behind his back, ready for action, thinking that we were unaware of his intention.

It's strange how often something that we're not supposed to do takes on a real attraction. It's the 'diet versus plate of chocolate biscuits' syndrome. We know that in order to lose weight we have to avoid eating fattening foods like chocolate biscuits. Unfortunately, although this is perfectly clear as far as logical argument goes, there is another, stronger force at work inside us, the part that really, really wants to do what it knows it shouldn't.

You know you should just walk away, but instead you keep looking at the plate and imagining the delicious chocolatey taste, and a little voice pipes up inside your head: 'Just one won't do any harm. You can always start again tomorrow.'

If you're not feeling particularly strong-willed at that moment, you may well find your resolution crumbling and before you know it you've eaten not just one biscuit, but two or three.

Temptation is subtle. It would be easy to withstand if we knew when it was coming, but often it attacks us when we're at our lowest ebb. Don't expect Satan to fight fair—he won't. Leave an area unguarded and that's where he'll concentrate his attack.

We may attempt to excuse the slip-ups we make. 'Oh yes, I watched that programme but it was only a one-off.'

'I know I shouldn't have behaved like that but I won't do it again.'

The problem is that although wrong behaviour may start off as an occasional lapse, if we're not careful it can become a habit and then a whole lifestyle.

Giving a cute, cuddly tiger cub the freedom of your home may not seem like a big deal, but wait until that cub grows up into a large powerful adult! Something that didn't cause too many problems in the early days can quickly get out of control once it reaches full strength, and can even maim you in the process. Don't introduce tigers into your life!

This is what happened to Eve (Genesis 3:6). She let something into her life that would break up her relationships, drive her out of the beautiful paradise where she'd been so happy, and ultimately destroy her.

As for so many of us, the root cause was that Eve craved something she was not supposed to have. God had given Adam and Eve permission to eat freely of every other fruit in the garden, but for Eve that was not enough. She wanted to taste the one fruit that was forbidden.

I suspect that long before the serpent came along, she had begun to wonder about the forbidden fruit, what it smelled like, what it tasted like, and the cracks in her armour were already there.

Are we like Eve, treading on dangerous ground—wanting something that we know we shouldn't have, something that God's word tells us is wrong? Is it causing us to waver in our faith, to allow doubt to creep in? 'Has God said…?'

Eve knew what God had said, but it didn't stop her looking with longing eyes at the forbidden fruit. From there it was downhill all the way—allowing herself to be persuaded by the wily serpent, reaching out and touching the fruit, picking it, holding it in her hand and finally taking that first bite.

Falling into sin is usually a gradual process. We know we should keep away, but something draws us closer and closer. If we do not resist and break free in the early stages, we can find that, like Eve, step by step we tread a path that leads inevitably to disaster.

Sinning did not bring Eve joy. It was only after she had taken the bait that she discovered the hook. What she had thought was so much to be desired brought tragic consequences that would only finally be resolved in Jesus' death on the cross.

When we sin there is always a tendency to shift the blame elsewhere, and Adam and Eve did just that (Genesis 3:12–13).

'It wasn't me. It was the serpent,' said Eve.

'It wasn't me. It was the woman *you* gave me,' said Adam.

'It wasn't me. It was my upbringing… something in my genetic makeup… the group I was with at the time.'

We often like to depict ourselves as helpless victims, unable to do anything about the situation, but we have to stop making excuses.

Eve could have turned away from the forbidden fruit. 1 Corinthians 10:13 says very clearly that we do not need to give in to temptation: 'God is faithful, and he will not let you be tested beyond your strength, but with the testing he will also provide the way out so that you may be able to endure it.'

We do not have to fall into sin. We can walk away from the temptation to get into an unrighteous relationship, to cheat in our workplace, to pass on gossip.

Sin deeply grieves God's heart, but his love for us goes deeper still. In the garden of Eden, Adam and Eve hid from God, bowed down by the guilt and shame of what they had done.

What was God's response? The relationship was broken because of their disobedience. Did he decide to have nothing further to do with them?

No, he 'called to the man' from a Father's heart of love: 'Where are you?' (Genesis 3:9). It's the same cry of love that he's been repeating ever since, ultimately sending his Son to die for our sins so that we can be restored to intimacy with him once more.

'Where are you?'

He is looking for us now, wanting to draw us close to him.

'Here, Lord.'

Looking inward / looking outward

Using a microscope can be a marvellous experience when you see the pigmentation and feathery texture of a butterfly wing or the serrated tree-trunk appearance of a single human hair.

However, it's not such a good idea to focus on the details of our lives so closely that we can no longer stand back and see the whole picture. Having an inward-looking perspective can bring distortion and magnify the problems we face, out of all proportion.

The Israelites experienced this when they sent twelve spies into the land of Canaan, the land flowing with milk and honey that God had promised them when he took them out of slavery in the land of Egypt: 'I will bring you into the land… I will give it to you for a possession' (Exodus 6:8).

However, in spite of God's promises and the richness of the land, the spies were divided in their opinion as to what they should do next. Ten of the twelve men had serious misgivings.

They had seen how fertile the land of Canaan was. They had even brought back a bunch of grapes so large that it had to be carried on a pole between two men. Unfortunately it was not just the grapes that were larger than normal. 'All the people that we saw in it are of great size,' they told the people, '…to ourselves we seemed like grass-hoppers, and so we seemed to them' (Numbers 13:32–33).

The ten fearful spies looked at the fortified cities and the strength of the opposition from an inward-looking perspective. Instead of viewing the land in the light of God's promises, they saw it through the distorting lens of their own limitations. Faced with a situation where the balance appeared to be heavily weighted in the enemies' favour, their advice was, 'Don't take them on—we're simply not strong enough.'

They were mentally defeated before the battle had even begun. They could see only the problem, not the solution.

Have you ever felt like a grasshopper when faced with certain people or situations—weak, small, and liable to be stepped on unless you are careful to keep out of the way?

How many times have we thought about facing up to a challenging situation or relationship and suffered from one of the 'in' words caused by inward looking—*in*adequacy, *in*security, *in*feriority?

Have you ever found yourself thinking, 'I could never have the courage to disagree—no one would listen to my viewpoint' or 'I just haven't got the confidence to do it. I'd like to, but I know I'd fall flat on my face'?

Inward looking—looking at all the ways we might fail, rather than thinking, 'Yes, I sense this is from God. I'll go for it with his help even though I feel shaky inside.'

We need to be outward-looking, like Caleb and Joshua. They were in a minority group of two, but that didn't bother them. Instead of focusing inward on their weaknesses, they chose to look outward, beyond their own capabilities, and to believe what God had said about the situation. What they saw was exactly the same as the other ten spies, but they did not view it through a lens of introspection.

'These people are giants,' moaned the ten spies.

'Do not fear the people of the land' was the response of Joshua and Caleb. 'The Lord is with us' (Numbers 14:9).

We are weak, fallible people, but just like Joshua and Caleb we have all the resources of heaven at our disposal:

- 'By my God I can leap over a wall' (Psalm 18:29).
- 'I can do all things through him who strengthens me' (Philippians 4:13).
- 'See, I am the Lord, the God of all flesh; is anything too hard for me?' (Jeremiah 32:27).

Counter inward looking with outward looking, and choose to believe what God says instead of your fears. He will never fail you or forsake you!

Idols

Does anyone take idols seriously nowadays? Not where I live. We might occasionally use the word in conversation. 'She idolizes her son,' we might say, or talk perhaps of screen and pop 'idols', but only in a light-hearted way.

When I was fifteen, one of my friends adored pop idol Donny Osmond. She knew all his songs by heart and the walls of her bedroom were plastered with posters. And it didn't matter what you talked about, you could guarantee that somehow she would manage to mention Donny at least once! She even slept with a photograph of Donny beneath her pillow and kissed it before she went to sleep each night.

Of course we would concede that in some other cultures the word 'idol' takes on a far more serious emphasis, but not in our own. On journeys abroad we may have come across shrines to idols, some roughly carved from stone, some overlaid with precious stones and glittering metals, and have felt a faint sense of superiority, because of course we don't practise such things in Western society, do we?

Idols? Surely that's all past history. It's the 21st century now. You won't catch us setting up golden calves or bronze serpents or images of other gods. We're far too sophisticated.

Twenty-first-century idols may not be physical images but they are none the less real. It's just that the packaging is slicker and it may take us a while to recognize them for what they are.

Take a good look around you. What is being worshipped in our society? You will see certain images paraded over and over again, certain creeds followed.

Some people deny the need to worship anything, but if you scratch beneath the surface you will find that everyone is, in fact, following their own 'religion', although of course it will go by another name—politics, materialism, the pursuit of success or beauty.

Idols are deceptive. They can appear relatively harmless—after all, they are created and put into place by human agency. They may even be beautiful, like the golden calf (Exodus 32:4), lulling us into a false sense of security.

I'm sure Solomon initially thought that there couldn't be much harm in allowing some of his foreign wives to set up idols within his court—after all, he was a servant of the living God. Big mistake! By the end of his life, Solomon himself was worshipping at the altars of these false gods (1 Kings 11:4–8).

Christians today can be just as easily deceived as Solomon. We allow something to take up residence in a corner of our lives, and then it becomes more and more dominant until finally it occupies centre stage and God is pushed to one side. I've seen it happen many times—haven't you?

A good definition appears in the Oxford English Dictionary. An idol is an 'object of excessive devotion' and to idolize is to 'love to excess'.

Is work your idol? Are you married to the job, constantly thinking about how to climb the promotion ladder or earn a bigger salary?

What about materialism? Have you become a worshipper at this popular 21st-century shrine where status is conferred by what we possess?

Love. What could possibly be wrong with love? Surely it's the highest human emotion? Beware: there's healthy love and unhealthy love. A love that totally dominates your life can carry in it the seeds of destruction.

There is no doubt that idols possess power over their worshippers. 'Follow us,' they say. 'Bow before us and you will receive your heart's desire.'

False gods—false promises. Idols have a bad habit of letting you fall flat on your face just when you need them most, as Jezebel and her prophets found in 1 Kings 18:27.

It was in vain that the prophets prayed and petitioned and wailed. Their god was a false god. There was no answer. 'He is meditating, or he has wandered away, or he is on a journey, or perhaps he is asleep and must be awakened,' taunted Elijah.

It's the same with the idols that we set up. Look at the big three—money, sex and power. They seem to possess huge influence and the promise of security, but you only have to follow the news to see how often their followers come to grief.

God is not like that. He is steadfast in every situation and will not abandon you when the going gets tough.

An idol exists only to be worshipped. It demands more and more of your life without ever filling the hollowness within, but the true living God wants a relationship with us, and our worship has no value unless it is freely given.

A shattered idol is no bad thing. For my friend there came a point when she no longer swooned at the sound of Donny's voice, and felt embarrassed at the mere thought of kissing his photograph. Her eyes had been opened.

Jesus tells us plainly, 'No one can serve two masters' (Matthew 6:24). Where there are idols in our lives, we need to tear them down ruthlessly.

Is there something or someone in your life that is exerting an unhealthy influence, something that little by little has crept into the place where God should be? Lay it before God now.

❖

Junk room

Most of us have an area in our house that we prefer not to enter or even think about. It's somewhere that we visit hastily, a place we're always glad to shut the door on, but none the less it is always there, lurking at the back of our mind, preying on our conscience because we know that we should, we really should, do something about it—but not just now!

Yours may be the garage or the garden shed, the cupboard beneath the stairs, the loft or even a spare bedroom. It's the place you hope none of your friends will ever see—the place where you keep all the junk.

It can get difficult to move in this area because of all the things that have been moved there for 'temporary' storage but have since taken up permanent residence, gathering dust.

If someone does stumble across your secret 'glory hole', you attempt to laugh it off. 'Oh yes,' you say apologetically, 'I'm going to clear it up...' to which the inner voice of truth adds its own postscript: 'This year, next year, sometime, never!'

And the pile just grows and grows and grows.

Recently I was sorting through one of these junk areas in our house (we have several!), and I was amazed by some of the stuff I came across. There were cardboard egg trays—a hangover from the time when our boys were little and 'making' projects were the order of the day—stacks of Christmas cards (well, the pictures were nice), a broken lampshade, and outgrown toys.

Then there were various bits and pieces that 'might just come in useful one day', including several punctured inner tubes, odds and ends of china, and outdated clothes—I'm hanging on to them just in case they come back into fashion!

A few things were useful, but most were just taking up much-needed space. Six dustbin liners later, the room's floor was visible once more and I felt wonderful. It was a task that I'd been putting off for months, but once I actually got down to it, clearing out all the junk wasn't nearly as difficult as I'd feared.

In our Christian lives, we too have areas where the door is firmly closed, places where we dump stuff that we're just not ready to deal with. We push it out of sight for the time being, and then conveniently forget about it.

What sort of things do we put in the junk room of our minds? Sometimes they can be feelings—feelings of hurt, perhaps, or reject-ion, anger or disillusionment. Rather than bringing them into the open and sorting them out, we choose instead to hide them away, and then wonder why we find it hard to praise God.

Sifting through my junk room, I came across a number of broken items. Some could be repaired, but others would have taken too much time and effort to fix so I consigned them to the rubbish bin.

However, God is the great repairer when it comes to things that are broken or damaged in our lives:

- broken trust—when someone you relied on has let you down badly
- broken relationships
- damaged confidence

Don't be afraid to hand such things over to the Maker of all things for repair and restoration. He is very gentle and his hands are the hands of a healer.

One additional bonus of my marathon clearing-out session was the finding of various mislaid items. It was a great joy to rediscover things I had missed, searched for and thought lost for ever, like my great-grandmother's casserole dish, found lurking in a corner, wrapped in several protective layers of newspaper. From languishing unseen, it now has pride of place in a glass-fronted cupboard where everyone can admire its beauty.

Precious treasures may also be hidden among the junk in our lives, just waiting to see the light of day, so keep your eyes open! The pressures of busy lifestyles may have caused things like a habit of daily prayer, time spent soaking ourselves in God's word or the ministry of befriending people and welcoming them into our homes, to be shut away, gathering cobwebs.

Now, as we clear out the clutter, we recognize afresh the beauty in these things, dust them off and bring them into regular service once again.

Junk is not good for us. It piles up around us and restricts our movement, our ability to grow. Life-junk may be:

- attitudes that we've outgrown but still hang on to because they're so familiar
- memories that restrict and inhibit us, keeping us living in the past rather than enabling us to live in the present and look to the future
- things that once had a vital part in our life but now are impeding our progress—dust gatherers, and relics that should have been thrown out long ago.

Clear out the junk and you will be amazed at the freedom it brings. Fling wide the windows of your soul and allow the breath of God to sweep in and refresh every part of you, including those areas that have been closed off for so long, those doors that you were afraid to open because of all the junk piled up behind them.

Breathe on me, Breath of God,
Fill me with life anew,
That I may love what thou dost love,
And do what thou wouldst do.

EDWIN HATCH (1835–89)

✤

Doing it my way!

Short cuts are great when they work, but when they don't they can be frustrating, time-consuming, even downright dangerous. I well remember one walk when we thought we could save a significant amount of time and energy by taking a different route to the marked footpath.

At first, all went well and progress was rapid, but soon we found ourselves negotiating a stretch of marshland, picking our way gingerly from tussock to tussock, occasionally missing our footing and sinking ankle-deep into rust-brown water. The clouds of mosquitoes buzzing round our heads didn't help matters either!

Although the road we were attempting to reach could be seen from where we stood, it took ages before we finally reached the comfort of its hard metalled surface. By this time our feet were soaked and tempers were short. 'Why on earth didn't we stick to the proper path?' Why indeed?

Before Abraham left Ur at the age of 75, God had promised, 'I will make of you a great nation' (Genesis 12:2). Three chapters later, however, Abraham is beginning to get a bit worried. After all, he and Sarah aren't getting any younger. Anxiously he reminds God of his promise: 'O Lord God, what will you give me, for I continue childless, and the heir of my house is Eliezer of Damascus?' (Genesis 15:2).

Once again God reassures him, 'Your very own issue shall be your heir' (Genesis 15:4). He takes Abraham outside and shows him the night sky, promising that one day Abraham's offspring will be as numerous as the stars sprinkled in the heavens. Comforted, Abraham believes that God will do as he has said.

For Sarah, however, it's a slightly different story. She is very much aware of her biological clock ticking away. Where is the son that God has promised? Perhaps Abraham misunderstood what God had said.

Have you ever found yourself in a similar predicament? Waiting is terribly difficult. You believe you've clearly heard God speak but nothing in your situation seems to be changing. As days, months and even years pass by, you wonder what on earth is going on.

Perhaps you feel that God has promised you a husband but it hasn't happened yet and you're getting tired of waiting for the right man. Or you were sure that God had promised you healing but the old aches and pains are just as bad.

The old serpent rears its ugly head once again: 'Has God said...?' Did he really say it or have we just been kidding ourselves all along? Is there perhaps another interpretation? Does it really matter how the promise comes about? Perhaps God wants us to use our own initiative.

Sarah couldn't bear the waiting any longer, so, like many of us, she decided to take matters into her own hands. She persuaded Abraham to take Hagar her maid as a wife—perhaps this would result in the longed-for baby.

Hagar did become pregnant with Abraham's child, but, far from bringing joy, the successful outcome of Sarah's carefully planned strategy resulted in nothing but grief and jealousy when Hagar began to despise her barren mistress (Genesis 16:4).

In one sense, Sarah's plotting had been successful. She got what she wanted, but instead of bringing blessing it brought friction—friction that continues to this day in the strife between Israeli and Arab nations.

What would have happened if Sarah had waited for God to act, if she hadn't seized matters into her own hands? She would have saved Abraham and herself a lot of unnecessary grief. Trying to 'organize' God never works, as Sarah found out to her cost.

In fact, it wasn't until, humanly speaking, all hope of a baby for Abraham and Sarah was long gone that God resolved their situation and fulfilled the promise he had given Abraham so many years ago.

When Sarah overheard the Lord saying that she would bear a son, her first reaction was incredulous laughter (Genesis 18:12), but I think that she had learnt an important lesson in the long years of waiting. Sarah knew that she had already tried to fulfil the promise through her own efforts and that she had failed miserably. She knew that she and Abraham could do nothing about it on their own.

By this time she had learnt wisdom. She knew that she had to step back and let God be God, to trust him and ignore the doubts.

I wonder how Sarah felt when the baby stirred in her womb. Did she think, 'What a fool I was not to trust God in the first place! Why on earth did I run ahead of his plans for me?'

Abraham's and Sarah's faith was rewarded by the birth of Isaac, whose name means 'laughter'. When we give our situations, however difficult, over to God and leave them in his hands, he brings joy into our lives.

We would like everything to be cut and dried, but God doesn't work like that. Sometimes prayers are answered immediately. At other times we grow weary because the answer seems so long in coming. Do not give up. Persevere!

God's timing is not our timing. God's timing is perfect.

❖

On yer bike

When I was a teenager I delivered newspapers using my mum's sturdy but old-fashioned bike. It was solidly built but had definitely seen better days. Awkward and cumbersome, it was hard work to pedal, especially with a heavy bag of newspapers.

Unfortunately my newspaper round was not a quick dash from house to house but a country route covering several miles. It included several steep hills, and it was in tackling these hills that I really longed for a newer bike.

Two of the gears no longer worked at all. The only one that did was the stiffest, and to make headway up any form of slope you had to stand on the pedals and push down with all your weight. Even then, the gear would sometimes slip, causing the pedals to spin freely round and make me suddenly lose my balance.

Another disconcerting habit of this old bicycle was that the chain would often come off—never when the sun shone and it would have been comparatively easy to fix, but only when it was pouring with rain or freezing cold!

However, I soon became an expert at getting the chain back on quickly and without getting oil all over my hands, which would have marked the papers and resulted in angry customers.

Over time, I grew accustomed to the old bike's eccentricities and the bike went wherever I went, all the time growing more and more decrepit and harder and harder to ride effectively. Finally it was obvious that it was time to invest in a new one.

Instead of utility black with patches of rust, the new model was painted a dashing metallic purple and was much lighter and easier to handle than the old heavy iron frame.

It was sheer delight not to have to contend with seized-up pedals and a split saddle shedding wads of stuffing. Instead I feasted my eyes on lots of gleaming chrome and, best of all, a choice of gears which would allow me to cope with most slopes with comparative ease.

On the old bike, it demanded so much effort to ride up anything but the gentlest of inclines that I would often get off and walk, pushing the bike beside me. Looking at the new bike, I couldn't believe my eyes—eighteen gears! No more walking up hills for me—unless they were very steep!

But it was when I actually went out cycling that I really noticed the difference. It was as if the new bike had wings!

The odd thing was that even though I had exchanged my old bike for a new one, I would often act as if I was still riding the old one. Because I had ridden the old bike for such a long time, my brain had got stuck in 'old bike' mode and sometimes found it hard to remember that now I could ride in a totally different way.

Old habits die hard. Forgetting that the new bike's gears were on the stem, I would automatically reach out to the handlebar, and when I came to a hill I would get off and start pushing before suddenly realizing that, on this bike, I didn't have to do that any more. Because of the extra range of gears, I could, if I wanted to, cycle straight to the top.

When we become Christians, God offers us a whole new dimension to our lives—in effect, extra 'gears' to help us cope with different life situations, like the gifts and fruit of the Spirit and the ability to praise God whatever happens.

Yet so often we act as if we haven't received these gifts. We wheel out the old bike with all its problems and ride around on it, wondering why everything is such a struggle, when all the time God's brand new model is at our disposal. Instead of using the new gears, which would enable us to progress with far greater smoothness, we find ourselves still reaching for the old habits and the old methods.

Different things can make us opt for the old way of life over the new. Sometimes we have a sneaking fondness for the old bike and we can't bear to get rid of it. After all, it's given us so many years of good service and at least we know exactly how it will behave in any given situation.

The new model is a bit of an unknown quantity. What on earth are all those different gears for, anyway? It's much easier and safer just to stick to those few that were on the old bike!

Or we may find it hard to believe that God is giving a brand new model to us because we don't really feel as though we've done anything to deserve it. And as for using it—we wouldn't dare. It's so beautiful, with its shining handlebars and glossy paintwork.

If we have a new bike, it is pointless if we just lean it against the wall and admire it. Bikes are for riding. It's the same with the newness of life that God gives us. He doesn't want us just to look at it from the outside and think how nice it is. He wants us to actually live in the fullness of it.

Riding the new bike may require a different set of skills that we don't possess when we first receive it. The things we were used to on the old one may have undergone adaptation or even be missing altogether, while there will be many innovative features that we haven't come across before. We need to learn what these new features are, and familiarize ourselves with how they work, so that we can make full use of all that God has given us.

As we continue riding the new bike, the things that at first we found strange or difficult will become second nature. We will know what gear to use when, and we may even find that, with practice, we can cycle all the way to the top of that demanding hill without getting off at all!

'So if anyone is in Christ, there is a new creation: everything old has passed away; see, everything has become new!' (2 Corinthians 5:17).

MISSING PIECES

✥

Missing pieces

In our family we always do a large jigsaw puzzle at Christmas time, leaving it out on a table so that when anyone has a few minutes to spare they can try to fit a few more pieces into the picture.

Different people have different techniques. Some people tackle the edge pieces first and build up the framework, whereas others like to find a recognizable part of the picture and work on that.

When you first get the puzzle out of the box, there are hundreds and hundreds of pieces jumbled together in the plastic bag which bear no resemblance whatsoever to the colourful illustration on the container. It is only as you fit the pieces together that the picture gradually appears.

Have you ever noticed how younger children will sometimes pick up a piece that looks as though it should fit into place, and when it doesn't, they try to force it in, becoming increasingly frustrated in the process?

Are we like that? Is there a part of our lives that we feel sure should be in a certain place? And if we discover that it doesn't actually fit, do we find that hard to accept? Instead of moving on and finding the right place for it, we just keep trying and trying to put it where we want it to go.

But it's never going to fit there, however much we want it to, if that is not the place that God has reserved for it. Trying to force a piece into place will not only damage the piece itself but possibly also the pieces surrounding it.

We need to stop banging our head against a brick wall and look instead for the right place, the one that God intended all along. When we have found it, we will discover that no force is required.

Some puzzle pieces are very smooth, but others are irregular and you find it hard to see how they are ever going to fit in. Such an awkward shape—what on earth was God thinking of when he designed a piece like that as part of our life structure?

How much easier it would be if all the pieces were like this one over here, smoothly formed with no awkward bits jutting out. We don't need to worry, though. It doesn't matter how irregular the shape may be, there is a matching gap for it somewhere within the puzzle.

It's not so difficult to fit pieces into the jigsaw when there's a lot of detail involved, as we can see fairly easily where such pieces belong in the overall picture.

It's much harder when we're working on an area made up of sky, containing a lot of very similar pieces without much variation. These are rather like the areas of our lives where we feel that nothing much is going on. Just another day at home or at work—in fact, very similar to yesterday and the day before—no great dramas or crises, no unexpected shocks or blessings.

Just routine, just another piece of sky—all blue with very little variation, each one having to be matched by shape because there's almost nothing to distinguish it from any of the other hundred or so pieces of sky.

The sky pieces in a puzzle may seem monotonous taken individually. They're all blue, all the same—but put them all together and they form a beautiful background to the picture and are just as important as all the more detailed pieces. Never discount those 'ordinary' days!

Probably the most frustrating thing when working on a puzzle is when you get so far with a section and then can't find the rest of the pieces needed to complete it. Sometimes just one crucial piece is missing.

When trouble hits us, we can't always understand what is going on. It just doesn't seem to make sense. We cry out to God, 'Why is this happening to me?'

Why are we suffering these life-storms? Where have these jagged holes come from that ruin the pleasant picture we were piecing together with such enjoyment?

Sometimes it can take months or even years before we can finally pick up the missing pieces and slot them into their respective places. When pieces are missing, it can be hard to see what certain parts of the picture actually are. Is that a tree or a person, or even part of a building? We simply don't have enough to go on, and until the missing pieces are in place we will not be able to see the whole picture.

Although for a time the picture we are forming may look broken and fragmented, that is not actually the case. It just hasn't been completed yet. The pieces are all there. They may have been mislaid for a while or even accidentally fitted into the wrong section, but they are still part of the picture.

God is the one who is working on the design that makes up our lives, and he knows exactly what the end picture will be. Everything that happens to us has a purpose, and while a particular situation may seem pointless at the time—a gap in the puzzle that we struggle to make sense of—it is actually a crucial part of the picture, and without it the picture would be incomplete.

We can rest secure because every piece belonging to the picture that makes up our lives is in the safest place of all—God's Father-hands. He knows exactly where to place the pieces, when, and in what order.

'For surely I know the plans I have for you, says the Lord, plans for your welfare and not for harm, to give you a future with hope' (Jeremiah 29:11).

❖

Pruning shears

We have a hedge at the bottom of our garden. When we first moved in, we worried that the trees were the ill-famed *Leylandii*, but in fact they are *Lawson's Cypress*, similar but more well-mannered. Even so, every two or three years the hedge needs trimming.

In past years, when money was short we sometimes tried to clip the hedge ourselves—a marathon undertaking as the trees are so tall and bushy. We soon discovered that it was almost impossible for us to cut the tops so that the line of growth was even along its length.

Have you ever tried to cut your own fringe? It's so easy to take a bit too much off one side, which you then have to try to match on the other. Then, just when you think you've finally got it right, you discover you've left one length much longer than the rest. Trimming a *Lawson's Cypress* hedge is just like that, but on a much larger scale!

The other problem with our trees was the sheer awkwardness of the task, trying to lop off branches growing at peculiar angles or branches that were just too large to remove easily.

After a few years, we decided that it was much easier to call in an expert than to try to deal with the problem ourselves. We just didn't have the necessary skills to do the job properly, and even after all our hard work, the hedge looked ragged and unkempt.

If we're honest, pruning in our Christian lives is not something that we look forward to. Let's face it—it hurts! We often try to avoid it by taking matters into our own hands. At least then if it gets too painful we can stop.

The problem is that it's almost impossible to see clearly when you're carrying out surgery on yourself. You get rather fond of some bits: 'Oh well, I don't think they're doing any real harm. Everybody else does it, after all.'

Or we may be far too hard on ourselves, allowing the perception of our weaknesses to cloud our vision and rob us of our joy, 'Look how I've just behaved. How can I even call myself a Christian?'

Actually the very areas we consider our greatest weaknesses may be seen quite differently through God's eyes.

Trying to prune our characters and bring them under control is a skilled task and not to be undertaken lightly. It's not as easy as it seems. Just think of all those New Year resolutions that people make every year. How long do most of those good intentions last?

In Jeremiah 10:23 the prophet observes, 'I know, O Lord, that the way of human beings is not in their control, that mortals as they walk cannot direct their steps.' God has his own schedule for our lives and if we try to seize the pruning shears from his hand, not only will we make a mess of the job—we may even hurt ourselves badly in the process. Pruning shears are a dangerous tool in the wrong hands.

For others of us, the temptation is not to bother with pruning at all, but to let things take their own course. However, this often leads to rampant uncontrolled growth. When my husband and I delay the process of trimming our hedge, it isn't long before pedestrians find their way obstructed by low-growing branches hanging over the pavement and call the overgrown trees to our attention.

Also, just across the road we have a constant warning in a similar hedge that has been left to grow unchecked with disastrous results. The trees—poor spindly things with thin trunks and sparse foliage—have shot skywards, and several have fallen because they lack the strength to withstand storms or strong winds.

Being left to our own devices is not good for us either. 'Oh, that's just me!' we excuse ourselves, but are our unchecked habits becoming obstacles to those around us? Without pruning, just allowing our own wishes and desires free rein, we will grow, but the growth will not be healthy.

However, pruning does not mean just hacking away regardless. The man cutting our trees is always very careful not to cut the branches back too far. Apparently, if you prune trees of this type too savagely, the green will not grow again and you will be left with unsightly brown, withered patches.

This is often the sad result of pruning undertaken by someone who may mean well but does not really know what they are doing. What should be beneficial actually harms and brings destruction.

If we have ever experienced the use of the pruning shears on our lives in unskilled hands, we know what pain can result, and that may cause us to flinch from future pruning.

We may feel that we simply cannot face the pain of the blade any more—we have suffered too much. There are too many brown patches in our lives already.

Take heart. God cuts only that which needs to be cut away, not for our harm but for our good, stripping out what holds us back—the diseased parts, the parts that have outgrown their strength or where the life-giving sap no longer flows.

Such pruning is still a painful process but often it's the only way for light to penetrate areas where branches have become knotted and twisted together. And it is when God's light shines into places that were once dark and overgrown that healing comes.

Heavenly pruning shears 'will not break a bruised reed or quench a smouldering wick' (Matthew 12:20). We can come to God with confidence and say, 'I'm willing, God, and I will not resist your sure touch. Prune what you need to in my life.'

It's the kindest cut of all.

✣

Leah

Can you imagine how Leah must have felt? Her relationship with her husband Jacob couldn't have had a worse beginning.

She was married to a man who didn't want her: he wanted her sister, Rachel. In the Revised Standard Version of the Bible, Genesis 29:17 is translated, 'Leah's eyes were weak, but Rachel was beautiful and lovely.' No prizes for guessing who would win the beauty pageant! Leah had grown up knowing that her younger sister was far more beautiful. It was hardly surprising that Jacob had fallen in love with her.

In order to marry Rachel, Jacob was willing to work for Uncle Laban for seven long years, but it seemed 'only a few days because of the love he had for her' (Genesis 29:20). Truly a labour of love!

At last it was time for Jacob's reward—the marriage day when he and Rachel would finally be united. There was just one problem. Jacob found that he had married the wrong woman. His new wife wasn't his beloved Rachel. It was her weak-eyed older sister, Leah.

What a shock! It's hardly surprising that he reacted to Laban's trickery with anger.

Poor Leah. She was left in no doubt that, as far as Jacob was concerned, she was no substitute for her beautiful younger sister. Marriage for her was not a joyful occasion and a celebration of mutual love. Instead of being a cherished and deeply loved bride, Leah was rejected from the outset. What a start to married life!

Leah could not walk away from the situation, either. She was not moving away with her husband to another place where perhaps she might have had the chance to make him forget the more attractive contender for his affections.

She would have only seven days with Jacob before her rival came on the scene, and then every day Leah would have to live with the knowledge that she was second best. She was under no illusions as to which sister Jacob preferred, and it was obvious to everyone else too. Genesis 29:30 states, 'He loved Rachel more than Leah.'

Leah found this hard to come to terms with. More than anything else, she longed for Jacob's love.

It wasn't a fair situation. Leah was in an unhappy marriage through no fault of her own. She was an innocent victim, manipulated by her father Laban. What could she do? If she went back to her father, she would suffer all the shame of a rejected wife. Even if she got rid of Rachel in some way, there was no guarantee that Jacob would love her.

However, there was one thing that Leah had that Rachel didn't—the ability to have children.

God had seen Leah's forlorn state and showed her compassion by opening her womb. While Rachel remained barren, Leah discovered that she was expecting a baby. Perhaps now she could take her rightful place as Number One wife.

Leah's first four pregnancies indicate the struggle she went through emotionally and her deep desire to gain the love of her husband. You can feel the triumph as she names her first son Reuben—'See, a son!' Perhaps there was an element of boasting here too: 'I can do something *she* can't!'

The next baby arrived at a low point in Leah's life. She had hoped so much to gain her husband's love through Reuben's birth, only to find that nothing had changed.

Leah called the new baby Simeon—'has heard'—because 'the Lord has heard that I am hated'. At this point the full bitterness of her situation was affecting her and she was suffering from self pity: 'Nobody likes me, everybody hates me!'

Son number three and still Leah desperately hoped to win Jacob's affections. 'Levi' actually means 'joined' and Leah hoped that this third son would finally unite her to Jacob. We can sense the desperation— 'Perhaps this time it will work.' There is a sense of ceaselessly striving to be loved, to be valued.

But then there comes a change. Leah has done everything in her power to change the situation but it has not altered. So what does she do then? Does she become a bitter, frustrated woman?

Interestingly, in these tough circumstances Leah has never given up on God. She has never ceased to bring her problems to him. She knows that even if she never succeeds in winning Jacob's heart, God is with her.

Of course God could have resolved Leah's situation, but he didn't. What he did do was to bring her to a place where she could leave the whole thing in his hands, resting in him.

God can do the same for us. When we are stuck in a situation that we can't change, God can change us so that we can deal with it. He will give us the grace and strength to cope, no matter how difficult the situation is or how long we've been going through it.

It doesn't matter whether it's cancer, troublesome teenagers, work problems, marriage difficulties or a host of other problems. God can bring us to a secure place in the midst of the storm.

This goes far beyond 'making the best of a bad job'. Paul wrote in Romans 8:35, 'Who will separate us from the love of Christ? Will hardship, or distress, or persecution, or famine, or nakedness, or peril, or sword?' God is with us no matter what happens, and if we hand our lives into his care, the turmoil of the waves and the lashing of the rain will no longer trouble us because his love and peace surround us.

Leah strove to win Jacob's love but finally she came to a place of acceptance, of trusting God for her future, however it might turn out.

When she gave birth to her fourth son, she was no longer trying to score points in competition with her sister or bewailing the harshness of her lot. She now recognized that God was in charge of her destiny.

Leah learned to look to God in the midst of her problems, and God himself became her strength. Nothing outwardly had changed. Jacob still loved Rachel best, and always would, but Leah had discovered the key to joy in difficult circumstances.

Her fourth child was named 'Judah'—'Now I will praise the Lord!'

✤

Paralysis of analysis

'Why is the sky blue?'

'Does God have a beard?'

'Where do babies come from?'

Small children love to ask questions—ask any mother! From a very young age there's an inborn desire to make sense of the world in which we live, to find out exactly how it works.

That doesn't change as we grow older. We love to be able to place everything in a labelled compartment in our minds. It gives us a sense of security and makes us feel as though we are in control of our lives.

If someone said, 'I'm going to send you hundreds of miles up into the air in a metal box travelling at a very great speed', we might feel worried. But if that box is called a 'plane' we quite happily undertake the flight because it forms part of our framework of understanding.

However, when we become Christians, we move into a different dimension from the one we were born in, and often we find it difficult to cope with the change.

God is not easily classified, we cannot slot him into a convenient filing system, and he often works in ways that we find hard to understand. 'For my thoughts are not your thoughts, nor are your ways my ways,' says the Lord' (Isaiah 55:8).

We would love it if the Christian life could be lived according to an instruction book like the one we use for the washing machine—if, when we pressed a certain button, we could guarantee a certain result. We are so used to our rational ways of thinking, in which $1 + 1 = 2$, that we find it difficult to get used to heavenly arithmetic where 5 loaves and 2 fish = enough food for a multitude. It just doesn't make sense, humanly speaking!

Our rationality can often prove a real stumbling block. When faced with a sticky situation we often try to solve it through our own efforts. Our minds go into problem-solving mode. 'It'll work out if I just do this, this and this…'.

We leave God out of the equation and only turn to him as a last resort when all else fails. Let's face it—the realm of faith is not our natural dimension and we struggle with it.

Martha found the same problem, even though she enjoyed a close relationship with Jesus and believed that he was the Messiah. When Jesus came to Bethany after Lazarus' death he and Martha had one of those conversations where the message simply isn't getting through.

Jesus was gently trying to bring Martha to a point of faith where she could believe that Lazarus would rise from the dead, but because her mindset was limited to everyday expectations, Martha totally missed the point.

She had no problem believing that if Jesus had arrived while Lazarus was still alive her brother would not have died. She also added, 'But even now I know that God will give you whatever you ask of him' (John 11:22).

It sounds like a great statement of faith. We too would say the same: 'Yes, Lord, I believe you can do anything!' But what happens when it's our own faith that's on the line? How easy is it then to trust God?

'Yes, I know you can do miracles, Lord, but...'. Somehow we rule out our own situation. Miracles—yes, fine. I believe that other people experience them, but me? I'm just not sure. In fact, I won't even ask for one in case it doesn't happen!

Jesus told Martha that Lazarus would be raised from the dead, but Martha's common sense stopped her from hearing what he was actually saying because from her viewpoint it was impossible.

Even when Jesus prompted her, 'Do you believe this?' and Martha answered 'Yes', it is obvious that she thought he was talking just in theoretical terms. She had no expectation that he was talking about something that was actually going to happen.

At the tomb, when Jesus told them to move the stone away, practical Martha reacted with horror: 'Lord, already there is a stench because he has been dead for four days' (John 11:39).

Poor Martha. She was standing beside the Lord of Life and still she could not move beyond the mental boundaries constricting her. Her mind would not let her believe. Her brother was dead—end of story.

The voice of reason says, 'No, don't do that—you'd be crazy to do that! Don't roll the stone away—there'll be a stink!' It takes courage to go against the flow, but fortunately for us the history of Christianity is full of crazy people who were bold enough to move away the stone, pushing the restrictions of human understanding to one side, and allowing God to work.

Our God is not limited by the human mindset that likes to compartmentalize actions into 'sensible' or 'not sensible'. In fact, very often God will tell Christians to do things that seem foolish in human terms.

Was it sensible for Jackie Pullinger to buy a long-distance boat ticket, not knowing where she was going to get off? How irresponsible!

Was it sensible for Elisabeth Elliott to move back with her little girl to the Auca tribe that had killed her husband?

Of course not! Yet God moved powerfully in these situations and many more, simply because people were willing to move beyond the constrictions of their minds and let God be God.

Romans 12:2 says, 'Do not be conformed to this world, but be transformed by the renewing of your minds, so that you may discern what is the will of God.'

Starting to live in the spiritual dimension is exciting—it's a place where literally anything can happen.

Water can turn into wine.

Lame men leap for joy.

A dead child breathes again and hugs her parents.

No, humanly speaking it doesn't make sense... but God does!

In times of drought

Some years back, I remember, there was an exceptionally hot dry summer when the River Stour, that normally flowed strong and deep across the fields, became so shallow that you could walk across the river-bed to the other side.

The grass was no longer fresh green but a dull brown, the earth parched and cracked, while the bracken in the forestry plantation was so tinder-dry that fire was a constant threat. One of the most poignant sights, however, was the limp, bedraggled body of a dead swan, its graceful head trapped inside a tin can as water levels in the river fell.

There's something about drought that deeply distresses us, perhaps because we know that drought is not a natural state. It is not the way that things should be.

Drought is the absence of life-giving water. Without water, the earth becomes dry, providing insufficient moisture for plants to thrive. Instead they wither up and die. In the most severe conditions, lives of animals and people will be lost. Who can forget the disturbing images of famine seen in newspapers and on the television screen?

Spiritual drought is perhaps less obvious, but no less serious. Jesus describes the natural condition of a Christian as one in which it is as though there are rivers of living water within. If those rivers dry up and cease to flow, spiritual drought is experienced, making healthy growth difficult or even impossible.

Have you been there? In dryness and barrenness, wondering where God is and how you got into this state in the first place?

There are two possible responses to spiritual drought. One is to accept the situation and try to forget what it was like to experience the river in all its fullness. We can eventually get used to being dried out, so that for us this becomes the norm and we adapt to it.

To do this, we produce fewer leaves and little or no fruit, and our growth is stunted. We can even come to like drought, and to feel threatened if we see the promise of rain. Rain would make us grow, and growing demands effort—it can even be painful. Actually we'd rather stay as we are.

Or the dry state in which we find ourselves can create a deep thirst within us for something different, something more. We're not satisfied with being dried out. We cry out desperately to God for relief, like David in Psalm 143:6: 'My soul thirsts for you like a parched land.'

Being thirsty is not just wanting a drink. There is an urgency, a passion about it. When you are really thirsty, it is all you can think about—how water looks, how it tastes, the cool feeling as you swallow it, the refreshing moisture.

The problem with drought is that it doesn't happen overnight. It's a gradual process, and you may not even notice how dry you have become and that it is time for a fresh infilling.

When we're thirsty, it's no good sitting with an empty glass in our hand, hoping that somehow it will fill itself. We have to actually bring the glass to the water source in order for it to be filled. We don't just stare at the tap and think, 'Water. Water.' We turn the tap on so that the water fills the glass.

When you're thirsty, you don't just take a few polite sips—you drain the cup dry. A few sips will moisten your lips but it won't quench your thirst. To do that, you have to really drink, to empty the glass and maybe even fill it again.

If we've been a long time without receiving from God, we need to come back to him and soak ourselves in his presence. When a plant has completely dried out, there is only one thing to do and that is to totally immerse the pot in water—a quick sprinkling from a watering can won't do.

One of the most amazing things about God's living water is that it doesn't matter how withered and dried up we've become, or how long we've been in this state, we only have to come to the spring of living water to be totally refreshed and restored. 'Though its root grows old in the earth, and its stump dies in the ground, yet at the scent of water it will bud and put forth branches like a young plant' (Job 14:8–9).

Are you living in drought conditions? Is living water welling up within you, sparkling and refreshing, or has it become a trickle?

Thirstiness is a good quality in a Christian—not being content but wanting more of God. Are you content with just a few sips, a quarter-glass, a half-glass or are you really drinking?

Are you thirsty? Come and drink.

True grit

Have you ever handled a rope of pearls? They seem to possess an inner light of their own, a moony radiance, and each pearl is a perfectly formed sphere. No wonder they have been so prized by beautiful women over the centuries.

It is hard to imagine that there could be any relationship between such a beautiful object and grit—insignificant little pieces of matter that are easy to overlook. There's nothing attractive about grit. You certainly wouldn't find it taking pride of place in a ballroom.

And yet without the grit there would be no pearl.

If you come into close contact with grit, you will find that it is not a very pleasant substance. At best it is irritating, at worst it can be extremely painful. A piece of grit in your eye hurts out of all proportion to its size.

It's hard for us to see the point of grit. It hurts. It's annoying. It's unpleasant. Nobody really likes it. It's just something that comes into our experience from time to time.

How we would love to have grit-free lives—lives that progressed smoothly with no trace of difficulty or pain.

We find grit hard to tolerate because it comes into our lives through no fault of our own. It's not something we've ever asked for or wanted. It is a foreign body—something that shouldn't be there.

Another annoying thing is that we have no control over grit. It comes without warning, often when we're already feeling weak, and disrupts the smooth running of our lives, causing anything from minor irritation to searing pain. The sharp, ugly little particles have a way of working their way into areas where we are most vulnerable and where they can cause maximum discomfort.

Before the days of cultured pearls, the finding of a pearl was an incredibly rare occurrence, and people spent enormous time and effort to find one of these costly treasures.

Divers would be hired to harvest the oyster beds and bring the dark oyster shells to the surface for examination, opening each one with care. There was no way of telling whether there was a pearl inside an oyster shell. They all looked exactly the same from the outside. A diver might have to search a thousand shells before finding what he was looking for—that elusive lustrous object.

Oyster shells are not terribly attractive in themselves. You would not expect the dark, rather ugly shell to play host to the beautiful, round, glistening pearl.

What makes the oyster create the pearl? You would expect some wonderful substance to be involved. The last thing you'd think of would be irritating, painful grit.

What happens is that a particle of grit becomes trapped inside the oyster shell, setting up an irritation. The oyster cannot get rid of the grit particle so it begins to coat it instead in layer after layer of nacre, the mother-of-pearl substance that will eventually become the pearl.

The pearl is totally different from the grit that triggered its formation. It is a perfectly smooth sphere with no sharp edges to cut or irritate. Where grit is dull and uninteresting, a pearl is beautiful and shines with light. Two objects could not be more dissimilar, but the one could not come into existence without the other.

'Grit' in our everyday lives is hard to tolerate, whether it's minor irritations—a difficult work colleague, stressful teenagers or a baby who won't sleep—or major setbacks like ill health or family tragedies. Nobody enjoys it when they're going through difficult times, when the grit is eating into tender flesh. 'Take it away!' we cry. 'I just can't stand it any more!'

The end result of the constant irritation within the oyster shell is something priceless, of great beauty, and God can transform us into people who, even in the midst of the most trying circumstances, radiate his light.

The great 19th-century missionary Hudson Taylor wisely said, 'It doesn't matter, really, how great the pressure is. It only matters where the pressure lies. See that it never comes between you and the Lord— then, the greater the pressure, the more it presses you to his breast.'

We can leave the grit as grit, allowing it to irritate us and even cause serious damage or we can ask God for the qualities we need to change the grit into something quite different, something precious.

Pearls in their natural state aren't easy to come by. That is why they are so highly valued. A pearl is not an overnight wonder. It takes many years for the layers to build up, and in the initial stages it looks nothing like the luminous sphere it will one day become.

Grit creates a flaw, and yet, as God's grace washes over us again and again, building up layer after layer of the fruit of the Spirit—self-control, peace, patience, kindness—the irritation is smoothed away.

Unlike grit, a perfect pearl is without any imperfection: its surface is without spot or flaw. The mother-of-pearl substance has smoothed over the original sharpness of the foreign body until it is as if it had never existed.

The ugly, jagged grit, with all its power to harm and disfigure, has become something quite different—a beautiful, smooth, perfectly formed pearl—something very precious in God's sight.

❖

At the tomb

The events of the last few weeks had been an emotional rollercoaster. It didn't seem possible that a situation could change so quickly and so dramatically.

One minute the crowd had been enthusiastic in their support, waving palm branches and shouting, 'Hosanna in the name of the Lord!' as Jesus made a triumphal entry into Jerusalem. They'd treated him like a king.

Yet just a short time later the mood of the crowd had turned ugly and they'd been baying for his blood. When Pilate tried to release Jesus because he found him innocent of the charges brought against him, the crowd would have none of it. 'Crucify him! Crucify him!' they'd yelled.

Then had come the darkest hours of all, when Jesus had been taken away to be crucified.

Mary Magdalene had seen the whole thing. She hadn't been able to take it all in. Surely this couldn't be happening—not to Jesus. It must be some awful nightmare—if only she could wake up.

How could she bear to see him die like this, the man whom she believed to be the Son of God—the man who had come into her life, opened the prison doors and set her free to live life in all its fullness?

How could she stand the dull thudding sound as the nails were hammered into his flesh? But Mary was determined not to leave him. She wouldn't turn away, she would stay to the end.

She heard his words, 'Father, forgive them; for they do not know what they are doing' (Luke 23:34). How like him, even as his body hung bruised and battered on the cross, to show love to those around him.

She waited. Perhaps even now something would happen. She had seen so many miracles. Jesus had raised Lazarus from the dead. She watched eagerly for angels to rescue her Lord. Surely this wasn't the end—it couldn't be. 'Father, into your hands I commend my spirit' (Luke 23:46).

It wasn't until the soldiers began to take down the body that the bitter truth hit Mary. There would be no miraculous deliverance. It was all over. She felt totally numb. Jesus—her Jesus—was dead.

Her last hopes vanished as the body was laid in the new tomb. Preparing the traditional spices to anoint Jesus' beloved body for burial, Mary was forced to face facts. Jesus was gone—for good.

Mary Magdalene must have been an emotional wreck by the early hours of the first day of the week when she returned to the tomb where they had laid Jesus.

She came heavy-hearted, not expecting anything any more, resigned to the situation—only to find that all was not as she had left it. The massive stone sealing the tomb entrance had been rolled away.

Mary was beside herself with grief. Couldn't they leave his body in peace now that he was dead? Hadn't they done enough to him already?

She called Peter and John, who examined the tomb. The body wasn't there. It had gone. Only the linen wrappings remained.

Mary was distraught. While Peter and John returned to the others with news of the disturbed tomb, she stayed behind weeping. She felt a sense of utter bereavement. Now she didn't even know where his body was. They had even taken that.

John 20 tells us that as she wept, she looked into the tomb and saw two angels in white sitting where the body of Jesus had been, one at the foot and one at the head. They asked her, 'Woman, why are you weeping?'

She replied, 'They have taken away my Lord, and I do not know where they have laid him.' All she wanted was to find Jesus.

As she said this, she turned round and saw someone standing behind her. It was Jesus, but at this point she did not recognize him. He was the last person she was expecting to see. Her whole focus was on finding the dead body. After all, hadn't she watched him die, hadn't she prepared the spices for his burial?

Jesus repeated the question, 'Woman, why are you weeping? Whom are you looking for?' Not 'what', 'whom?'

But Mary was still looking in the wrong place for her Lord. Have you ever done that? Searched for God in all the wrong places and failed to recognize him because his answer did not take the form you were expecting—failed to realize that the whole time he was standing right beside you, just waiting for you to turn and recognize his presence?

Mary thought he was the gardener and again asked him where her Lord had gone.

Jesus' next word was a very simple one: 'Mary.'

How Mary's heart must have leapt as she heard Jesus call her by her name. Mary was used to listening to Jesus. She had followed him with her whole heart since the day she first met him. It was because she was so attuned to his voice that she was able to recognize it and make the leap of faith to the startling truth that the Jesus who had died in agony on the cross was here with her now.

Jesus sent her back to tell the disciples. Can you imagine how she felt? How the words, 'He's not dead! He's not dead!' must have sung in her heart. The news would have given wings to her feet as she ran back to the room of mourners with their eyes red from weeping, all hope lost—running, running, gasping out, 'I have seen the Lord!'

Those who heard her story found it hard to accept. Surely Mary's grief had affected her mind. How could she have seen Jesus? They knew he was dead. As far as they were concerned, Jesus had gone away and they were now alone. The stone that had sealed the tomb had also put an end to all their hopes. They thought it was pointless looking for Jesus.

We can experience similar difficult moments when we too despair of finding Jesus, when it seems that a stone has been rolled across our hopes, blocking out the light and preventing us from reaching him.

But don't despair. Keep watching. Keep listening. Have your ear attuned in readiness and you will catch the whisper of his voice when you least expect it.

We are not alone, whatever our feelings may tell us, however desperate the situation. We have only to listen carefully with our heart and we will hear his voice again.

He doesn't rebuke us for being so slow in recognizing him or get angry at our weakness. He doesn't forget our name like a busy schoolteacher, 'So here you are at last—um… er…'

He calls us individually by name, and as we turn at the sound of that beloved voice we realize that actually we were never alone—not for one minute. He was there all the time.

LOVE—A TENDER PLANT

❖

Love—a tender plant

When I was a student in London, I possessed a magnificent coleus plant. It was a mass of decorative foliage, with beautiful dark purple leaves splashed with gold and cream, and was one of my most prized possessions.

Because the stems of the coleus were fairly soft and could easily be damaged, I didn't want to risk taking it on the train journey back to my home during the summer holidays, so I decided to leave it with my fiancé.

The coleus was quite a delicate plant and needed to be kept away from draughts. In order for the bush to thrive, the compost also required careful watering to prevent it from drying out.

I positioned the plant carefully on the dining-room mantelpiece in my fiancé's flat where it would get just the right amount of light, tenderly watered it for the last time, and placed the spray bottle beside the pot where it would be easily accessible.

The evening before I was due back in London, my fiancé was washing up in the kitchen when one of his flatmates walked in, looking puzzled. 'Have you any idea what this is?' he asked, holding out a dusty pot with what looked like a dried-up stick in the centre.

Sadly, the withered stem was all that remained of my cherished plant. Without the care and attention it needed, it had died.

We can forget to look after something that looks as though it is already flourishing. Because it looks so good now, we assume it will always be that way—the leaves will remain fresh and vibrant and shoots will continue to sprout.

Unfortunately, it doesn't matter how bushy and luxuriant the plant is to begin with; if it doesn't receive ongoing care and attention it will eventually wither up and die.

Sometimes we make the same mistake with love. Love seems such a strong emotion that we assume it will last for ever with little or no attention, but nurturing is important for love too, not just for plants.

What exactly do we mean by this word 'love', anyway? Is it simply a gooey feeling inside, or something else? There are so many different types of love—love of parents for child, child for parents, boyfriend and girlfriend, husband and wife.

'Love' is a very popular word in today's society. We use it all the time, almost without thinking. 'I love jazz,' we might say, or, 'I love that dress you're wearing!' The word appears on thousands of greeting cards—or we might sign a letter, 'With love…'

The media find that the 'love angle' is a good selling point for their stories. People are fascinated by people in love and enjoy reading about them. Sadly, however, that love often seems very short-lived.

We're all familiar with stories in which one moment a famous couple are madly in love 'for ever', and yet, just a few years later, they go their separate ways. What happened to the love? Where has it gone? Can love wear out?

Love is one of the greatest things that we can ever experience, but it is also one of the most misunderstood. Many things that we call love are actually just self-interest masquerading under another name.

Another person's love for us is not to be manipulated for our own ends. This is something that women can be very good at. Delilah knew just how to get under Samson's skin. 'How can you say, "I love you," when your heart is not with me?' … Finally, after she had nagged him with her words day after day, and pestered him, he was tired to death' (Judges 16:15–16).

Have we ever behaved like Delilah to get our own way? Be honest!

Something else that women are prone to is conditional love, giving love if certain conditions are met and withdrawing it if they are not. This is love only on our terms. Michal loved David, but her love died when she felt that David was embarrassing her by inappropriate behaviour. She saw David 'leaping and dancing before the Lord; and she despised him in her heart' (2 Samuel 6:16).

Are there behavioural quirks, or certain character traits, that annoy us in those we love? Have we allowed critical attitudes to drive a wedge between us?

Withholding love has no place in the heart of a Christian woman.

Just think of all our faults and the fact that God still loves us passionately in spite of them!

Of course, the famous benchmark passage about love for Christians is 1 Corinthians 13:4–8.

Love is patient; love is kind; love is not envious or boastful or arrogant or rude. It does not insist on its own way; it is not irritable or resentful; it does not rejoice in wrongdoing, but rejoices in the truth. It bears all things, believes all things, hopes all things, endures all things. Love never ends.

Quite a list! Perhaps, reading it, we feel that we fall woefully short of those godly standards. In many ways, love is not natural for us, and this is why we find it so difficult. It's far easier to just look after Number One without having to consider others, but God has called us to something higher.

For a Christian woman, loving is not an optional extra—it's part of the package.

We need to learn to love when circumstances are difficult:

- when we're suffering from PMT
- when we feel misunderstood or hurt or rejected
- when our family tests our patience to breaking point
- when we're mixing with people that naturally we don't get on with

It's about commitment. If you love someone, you don't opt out when the going gets tough—you keep going.

Instead of acting in a self-centred way like Delilah and Michal, we can follow Ruth's example: 'Where you go, I will go; where you lodge, I will lodge; your people shall be my people, and your God my God. Where you die, I will die—there will I be buried' (Ruth 1:16–17).

That is love—laying your own rights aside and sticking with the other person, no matter what!

✤

Family heirloom

In my childhood home, pride of place was given to an old cupboard, a family heirloom that had been passed down from oldest son to oldest son for many generations.

It was a beautiful piece of furniture. The walnut had a richness and warmth created by years and years of diligent polishing, and a delicious pungent scent of beeswax and lavender.

However, in spite of its great age and value, the cupboard was by no means off limits. As a piece of furniture it had been created to be used, and continued to fulfil that purpose, even though it was now hundreds of years old. It wasn't an object to be just looked at, to be handled with care. This was a piece of furniture built for use, that had served for many years.

As you might expect, the cupboard hadn't escaped the passage of time without receiving its fair share of knocks and dents. When these marks were first made, they would have been raw and new, perhaps even seeming a blemish on the cupboard's surface.

As time passed, however, the chips and dents had been smoothed and worn down, darkening in colour, so that they were no longer so apparent and indeed added to the overall character of the piece.

All five of us children treated the cupboard with respect, even with a certain reverence. We knew that it wasn't like the other furniture in the house. There was something extra special about it.

Fetching something from that cupboard was a privilege. Turning the well-worn brass key in the lock and running your hand along the shelves with their smoothly rounded edges, the work of a real craftsman, was a delight.

The beautiful glowing patina of the wood, like the glossy skin of a conker when you prise it from the green, spiky casing, had in fact built up largely because of the touch of so many hands over the years. It was a much-used and much-loved piece of furniture.

Antique dealers recognize the beauty that comes with age and value it highly. Such a piece of furniture is likely to attract higher bids than its modern counterpart, however innovative the design.

Age is also something to be prized in God's eyes. Scripture is full of men and women who were 'heirlooms' in God's purposes. I think of Paul commending Timothy for his sincere faith in 2 Timothy 1:5—and where did that faith come from? It was 'a faith that lived first in your grandmother Lois'.

I think of Anna in Luke 2:36–38, certainly no spring chicken at the age of 84 but with a heart totally for God. She 'never left the temple', the place of God's presence, and 'worshipped there with fasting and prayer night and day'.

Anna obviously did not believe it was time to retire, to step back and leave everything to the younger women—she was still actively serving God with her whole being.

I think it was because of her wholehearted commitment and faithful service over many years that Anna was instantly able to recognize the seemingly helpless baby in the temple for who he really was.

You'd have thought that one of the temple leaders would have been the first to recognize the Messiah. After all, weren't they men of authority and power, well read in the scriptures, trained in spiritual disciplines?

But they missed it. Anna didn't.

A woman whose husband had died after only seven years of marriage, Anna had spent the rest of her life faithfully following her Lord, worshipping day after day in his presence and listening for his voice, so that when the insignificant baby appeared in the arms of a humble country couple, God was able to whisper to her heart, 'This is him. He's the Saviour of Israel.'

Anna's response was not to question, 'Are you sure, God? What's he doing here as a baby? I thought he was supposed to be a strong deliverer. Surely there's some mistake!' She immediately began to praise God and 'to speak about the child to all who were looking for the redemption of Jerusalem' (v. 38).

I think too of godly older women such as my godmother Joyce, who has been inspirational to me in my Christian walk—women whose faces have an inner radiance that transcends any wrinkles they might have acquired over the years, women who have weathered the storms of life and yet shine only the more brightly, continuing to trust in the living God.

They are God's heirlooms—women crowned with years and beautiful in spirit, fulfilled women reaping a harvest of years of faithful witness and encouragement, years full of fruit.

'You shall come to your grave in ripe old age, as a shock of grain comes up to the threshing-floor in its season' (Job 5:26).

❖

Love song

All this talk about kissing and flocks of goats, intoxication and vineyards—isn't it rather excessive? Where's the spirituality? It all seems a bit carnal to me.

The Song of Solomon (or Song of Songs) isn't an entirely comfortable book because it deals in excess. The love it talks about is not a shallow brook that we dip our toes into when we feel like it, but a raging torrent that sweeps us off our feet. It's a book that talks of passion, consuming passion—and passion is something that disturbs us.

The Song of Solomon woman is no shrinking violet either. She bursts on to the page and, without the decency even of an intro-duction, embarks on the subject that is most important to her: 'Let him kiss me with the kisses of his mouth!' (1:2).

One thing and one thing only drives this woman—her consuming passion for the Beloved. She cannot wait to be in his presence again. She lives for that moment and can think of nothing else.

The Song of Solomon woman is a woman who positively rejoices in her femininity and is not ashamed of her sexuality. She sees it as a gift, part of who she is—not something to be ashamed of but something to glory in. Nothing takes too much time or trouble as she seeks to express her love for the Beloved. She invests in costly herbs and spices, myrrh, frankincense, nard and cinnamon to add to her attractiveness. She does everything in her power to make herself beautiful for him.

There is a quality in the love expressed by the Song of Solomon woman that is almost reckless. She is not afraid to give herself totally.

Love is the ability to trust without reserve. Separateness, holding back, making sure that you don't give too much away, are all signs that ultimately you don't completely trust the other person.

The Song of Solomon woman is not like that. She makes herself vulnerable because she holds nothing back from the loved one. She wants to give every part of herself, to know and be known.

Intimacy is frightening. It demands sacrifice—a willingness to forget about our own self-importance, to let go and become immersed in the Beloved. No more pride, no more pretence, but reality—not being afraid to be who we are.

It's no mistake that God so often compares his love for the Church in terms of the love between a bride and a bridegroom. God is not content with anything less than a love relationship. He woos us tenderly and he wants us to respond.

He is not satisfied with a long-distance relationship where we never engage closely with him. He wants intimacy, and nothing else will do.

I can't imagine the Song of Solomon woman being content with only an occasional meeting with the Beloved—perhaps at the Wednesday house group or prayer meeting, or during the Sunday service. She wants to be with the Beloved all the time, where she can see him, hear his voice and touch him.

What sort of relationship do we have with the one we love? Is it a casual 'I'll see you when I see you' relationship, with no real commitment on our part?

Is it an 'I've got my own life to lead' relationship, where love is pushed to one side?

Is it a relationship without true intimacy, conducted through letters and phone calls, perhaps even with a good photograph of the Beloved that we like to look at, but which never seems to progress to a face-to-face encounter?

Is it a relationship of convenience—'I'll only call on you when I need something'?

Or is it like the love relationship of the Song of Solomon woman? Is there an urgency to seek out the Beloved, to come into his presence whenever possible?

Is there a sense of expectancy, of sheer delight when you know that you are going to spend time with him? Is he more important than anyone else? Is he the one you cannot live without?

Is there intimacy?

❖

Seeking God's face

When you have toothache, it's hard to believe that the great throbbing pain that seems to dominate the whole universe is caused by such a minor part of the body.

It's PAIN in capital letters, and however hard you try, you can't get away from it. Toothache won't let you relax, you can't enjoy your food, and as for sleep—forget it!

People with toothache can act very strangely. Some of us try to adopt the 'mind over matter' approach, hoping that if we ignore it the pain will just go away. We'll try anything rather than arrange an appointment with the dentist, and out come the painkillers, the oil of cloves, the hot-water bottles.

Eventually, however, the pain drives us to do something about it, and we pick up the phone and do what we should have done in the first place, an action which would have spared us hours of unnecessary agony if we'd only given in and done it sooner.

Will we never learn? At last we admit defeat and ring the one who can deal with the problem, the one who knows about teeth—the dentist.

God isn't just an expert on teeth. He knows us through and through. He even knows the exact number of hairs on our head. And yet, when we are in pain or suffering some deep crisis, where do we turn?

Sometimes, like the reluctant dental patient, we refuse to admit that a problem exists, going into denial, while all the time the pain of the wound bites ever deeper, becoming more infected the longer we leave it untended. Or, in contrast, we become totally swamped by what is happening and allow it to demoralize us and knock us off our feet.

If we do recognize that we need help, where do we go? Do we try to read up the subject in helpful books and articles, ask a friend's advice, maybe even book an appointment with our GP, a counsellor or minister?

It's amazing that, for so many people, God is actually the last resort rather than the first, as he should be.

Hannah didn't make that mistake. When she experienced a painful crisis in her life, she went to the temple, not to see Eli the priest but to lay her case before the living God himself (1 Samuel 1:9–11).

Hannah 'poured out her soul'. Most of us like to control the flow—perhaps a steady trickle, nothing too drastic—we're not comfortable with letting it all 'hang loose'.

Hannah didn't care whether her behaviour was appropriate or not. Like King David dancing before the Lord in 2 Samuel 6:16, she wasn't concerned that people might think her strange or odd. Eli actually thought she was drunk!

She had only one thought in her mind. Her whole focus was on meeting with God, coming into his presence, seeking his face. It was between her and God—nobody else.

Sometimes it is only in the place of brokenness, in the place where we come to the end of ourselves, that we truly discover God.

Hannah met with God and left the temple, a changed woman. Gone were the tears, the overwhelming sadness. She knew that God had heard and she left the situation in his hands. She let go.

God 'remembered' Hannah and she gave birth to the baby that she had wanted so much. After so many years of wrestling with the issue of her barren state, years of emotional pain and anguish, Hannah finally held the longed-for son in her arms.

But Hannah had made a promise and, even as she experienced the sweetness of motherhood, she did not go back on the vow she had made.

How could she do what she did next? Most women in her situation would have been tempted to hold on to that special baby, never letting him out of their sight.

So how could Hannah just give him away like that, leaving him in the temple with old Eli, and even singing a song of praise to God afterwards? (1 Samuel 1:28—2:10). Was she crazy?

After all, at this point Hannah didn't know whether she would go on to have any more children. For all she knew, Samuel might be the only child she would ever bear, but still she did not hold back.

When Hannah encountered God in her time of desperate need, something changed in her even before she found that she was pregnant. The God of all-sufficiency met Hannah in her deficiency and she would never be the same again.

Hannah had poured out her soul; she had sought God's face and experienced his touch of love. Although she deeply loved Samuel, Hannah was able to give him freely because she knew that the only reason Samuel was there was because God had given him to her in the first place.

It was a difficult choice to make but Hannah knew that ultimately she would not lose out in giving to God because he always gives back in full measure, 'pressed down, shaken together, running over' (Luke 6:38).

Hannah was a sacrificial giver. She gave to God what she cherished most, her heart's desire. She gave without regret and with no strings attached.

What about us?

Perfume

My grandmother had been a beauty in her youth and was still beautiful in old age, but the thing I remember most about her is the delicate scent of lavender that always clung to her person.

Even now, whenever I pass a lavender bush in a garden I can't resist rubbing the grey leaves or blue flower spikes, releasing the slightly pungent, spicy scent that for me immediately conjures up my grandmother's image.

The perfume she used was contained in a beautiful, ornate, cut-glass bottle that stood on the carved oak dressing-table in her bedroom. I loved to carefully remove the stopper and sniff the aromatic fragrance. Occasionally, for a special treat, my grandmother would let me dab a little on my wrists, and throughout the day I would be accompanied by the delicious, evocative scent of lavender.

Perfume is costly stuff. When you visit the cosmetic counter in a department store you will not find it sold by the litre. It is far too precious for that.

The creation of perfume involves the subtle blending of different ingredients in precise proportions to achieve the desired effect, and because of the degree of skill involved, some perfumes cost a small fortune. Such is the desirability of perfume that every woman knows the names of creators of famous brands—Chanel, Coty and Estée Lauder.

Even the cardboard packaging is designed to attract the eye and gives the message that what is inside is something very special indeed. The perfume containers inside the boxes are even more beautifully crafted and are often works of art in themselves.

If we are going out somewhere extra special, we will often reach for our favourite perfume. Usually we will apply it sparingly. Just a small amount is sufficient to envelop us in fragrance.

However, when Mary, the sister of Lazarus, used perfume to anoint Jesus' feet, she didn't use just a few drops. She used a whole pound of an extremely costly perfume made from pure nard, a rich and exotic ingredient.

Can you imagine what that must have smelled like? We read in John 12:3 that the whole house 'was filled with the fragrance of the perfume'. Everywhere you went, you would have been met by the most delicious fragrance.

It was a beautiful gesture but it met with anger. What a terrible waste! Why hadn't the perfume been sold instead and the money given to the poor? It cost the equivalent of nearly a whole year's wages for a labourer. What was the point in using it all at once, pouring it out like that? Where was the sense?

You can imagine the same question being asked of Jesus' death on the cross. What was the point of it all? How much more practical it would have been if Jesus had overthrown the Romans and taken up a position of power. But to pour out his life on the cross, the fragrance of his being—what senseless waste!

Perfume doesn't seem practical, but the thing about perfume is that it spreads, and objects that come into contact with it will then also become infused with fragrance. If you place sachets of dried lavender in drawers that contain clothing or bedding, those items will also become scented with lavender over a period of time.

When we are in close contact with Jesus, the fragrance that is in him will actually rub off on to us. 2 Corinthians 2:14–16 says, 'And through us spreads in every place the fragrance that comes from knowing him. For we are the aroma of Christ to God among those who are being saved and among those who are perishing; to the one a fragrance from death to death, to the other a fragrance from life to life.'

What a privilege that within us is distilled the fragrance of Christ himself. But what are we doing with this most precious of perfumes?

The purpose of fragrance is to be used. However beautiful the container, however delicious the fragrance, if the stopper remains in the bottle the perfume is useless. It might as well be cleaning fluid.

Are we guilty of admiring the fragrance that Christ has given us, thinking how beautiful it is and what a wonderful perfume it possesses, but never actually removing the stopper, so that nobody else ever gets to smell it?

Just imagine what would happen if all of us who have experienced the fragrance of Christ in our own lives stopped hugging it to ourselves, stopped keeping it firmly contained in our nicely cut, decorative bottles where no one ever sees it but ourselves.

What would happen if we all made a decision not to do that any longer, to throw caution to the winds, taking our courage in our hands, and to remove the seal, releasing the beautiful fragrance into a world that is literally dying for it:

- into our families
- into our homes
- into our places of work
- into our neighbourhoods

Releasing the sweetest scent of all, everything around becomes saturated, soaked in perfume like the fragrance in a garden after falling rain—the fragrance that comes from knowing Jesus, our Saviour and our Lord.

✣

Mother love

What are your favourite childhood memories of your mother? We recently held a party for my mother's 70th birthday. It was quite an event, with all her five children and their families gathered together for the occasion.

As part of the celebrations, we made a memory box which contained items linked to memories of Mum—things like a packet of Scott's porridge oats, because at breakfast time Mum used to run round the garden with the porridge saucepan to cool it quickly so that we children wouldn't miss the school bus.

There were sad memories, happy memories, things that made us laugh and things that brought tears to our eyes.

The Bible is full of examples of motherhood, both good and bad. The love of a mother is one of the most powerful influences in a person's life, and an awesome responsibility.

You can be a strength for good in the life of your child, like Hannah or Timothy's mother, both righteous women with a deep love of God, or an evil influence like Athaliah, the mother of Ahaziah. 2 Chronicles 22:3 notes sombrely, 'His mother was his counsellor in doing wickedly.'

It's interesting that part of God's plan for his own beloved Son, Jesus, involved a human mother, Mary, to nurture and care for him as he grew up into manhood. God obviously values motherhood highly.

Motherhood is a precious gift from God, but we must not make the mistake of limiting it to those who physically bear children. Being a mother can be a spiritual rôle as well as a biological one.

Deborah is described as 'a mother in Israel' (Judges 5:7). Does this mean that she produced lots and lots of children? Of course not, but it does mean that Deborah had the heart of a mother towards her homeland, and cared deeply about what happened to it.

The phrase 'a mother in Israel' is used again in 2 Samuel 20:19 with reference to a city called Abel. Can a collection of buildings be a mother? Yes, because Abel was a place of refuge where people could come to seek counsel and settle disagreements, a place where love was shown towards those who needed it.

In fact, motherhood in God's kingdom does not necessarily follow the pattern that we see in our human circumstances at all.

> *Sing, O barren one who did not bear;*
> *burst into song and shout,*
> *you who have not been in labour!*
> *For the children of the desolate woman will be more*
> *than the children of her that is married.*
>
> ISAIAH 54:1

Children for the childless, for the single woman? Yes, because being a mother in God's eyes is a heart attitude. You can be a spiritual mother to others, whatever your situation. It is a gift that we can all receive.

A good spiritual mum is not ambitious, but possesses a sense of vision for those she cares for, to see them reach their full potential in God. She is not over-possessive and smothering, but releases others, allowing them to spread their wings and leave the nest when the time is right.

She does not love selfishly, but selflessly.

She gives praise, not condemnation.

She is not afraid to set standards and reflects God's character in her behaviour.

God himself sets such a value on this sacrificial attitude of mother love that he uses it to describe the way that he feels about us. He talks of a time of blessing for Jerusalem in Isaiah 66:12,13:

> *You shall nurse and be carried on her arm,*
> *and dandled on her knees.*
> *As a mother comforts her child,*
> *so I will comfort you.*

This is a beautiful picture of the way that God wants us to relate to him, in the same way that a young child relies totally on its mother. Mother love is something infinitely precious.

Unfortunately, mother love is less common than it once was. Out there, the world is hurting. Many people have grown up without experiencing love, without being nurtured.

Who can touch these lonely, disillusioned people? Who will reach out to them?

God is looking for mothers—those who can minister his love, provide a listening ear, perhaps even a shoulder to cry on; those who will love people through thick and thin without counting the cost, offering them acceptance and encouraging them to become all that God wants them to be.

Could you be one of them?

WINGS LIKE AN EAGLE

❖

Wings like an eagle

When an eagle is learning to fly, it is a potentially hazardous experience, because eyries are situated so high up—some 1500 to 2000 feet above ground level. The drop is a scary one—daunting for the young bird that has never flown before.

The eyrie must seem such a safe place. Its high sides protect the eaglet, sheltering it from high winds and offering a place of refuge.

When we are in a place that is familiar to us, that we know well and have become accustomed to, there may seem little point in going anywhere else. Why should we? We're perfectly happy there—and just look at the superb view! We can see it just as well from inside the nest. Why should we venture outside?

We've heard that flying is wonderful, but we're not sure we want to try it. There's so little margin for error—and what about that drop! 'No, thank you very much, I'm fine here.'

Probably, the eaglets aren't terribly keen to leave the nest in the first instance. After all, it's all they've known up to that point. But the adult eagle is not prepared to let matters rest there. Gently but firmly she stirs the nest, forcing the eaglets to begin to use their wings to keep their balance.

Are you finding that your nest is being stirred, that the circumstances you thought so settled are being shaken, forcing you to try your wings and abandon the safety of the nest?

Flying is not easy when you're a novice or when you haven't flown for some time, and sometimes you need that nudge to make you take to the wing.

However, the eaglet is not just pushed out of the nest and left to get on with it. The adult eagle remains close at hand and, should a flying attempt begin to go disastrously wrong, the mother eagle does an amazing thing, actually carrying the struggling eaglet that has run into flight problems back up to the security of the nest.

There is a lovely verse in Exodus 19:4 where God describes himself in similar terms: 'You have seen what I did to the Egyptians, and how I bore you on eagles' wings and brought you to myself.'

With this assurance, we need have no fear when we launch out into previously untried flight areas. As long as we are flying in the direction that God intends, he will provide the safety net should we find that we have overreached our strength. And as our flight muscles grow strong, we will fly further, faster, truer, for that is the purpose of an eagle—strong, soaring flight.

I once saw an eagle in a zoo hunched on its perch, dusty and battered, one of the saddest sights I had ever seen.

This majestic bird, with an amazing wingspan of seven feet and capable of hurtling downwards like a feathered thunderbolt at speeds of up to 90mph, looked totally out of place in the cramped cage, hemmed in by bars and metal mesh. It looked completely and utterly bored. My heart bled for this beautiful bird that should have been soaring high on the wind thermals, king of the skies.

There is nothing sadder than an imprisoned eagle, unable to fulfil what it was created for, caged instead of free. We are meant to be eagles and yet sometimes it seems we voluntarily choose the cage rather than the opportunity to fly.

We know that as daughters of God we should be the freest of people but instead we cower inside self-created prisons. 'Oh well, I don't want people to think I'm strange or a fanatic' or 'I can't pray for that person. Suppose nothing happens?'

We allow ourselves to be shut in on every side, and one day, sadly, we find that we have lost the power of flight because we have not used the inheritance that is rightfully ours. It has been so long since we last exercised our wings that the muscles have grown weak and will no longer bear our weight.

Instead of soaring high in the air, there we are among the pigeons, trying to act like one of them. But while an eagle may spend all its time with pigeons, eat like them, walk like them, and even learn to sound like them, an eagle will never become a pigeon. It is just an eagle in the wrong place.

Yes, they are both birds and they can both fly. But the eagle has the ability to rise on the thermals, to catch the wind of the Spirit and be lifted by it.

So which will we choose to be?

Will we remain an eagle that is behaving like a pigeon, head down, eyes to the ground, keeping in with the crowd, flying only when the rest do and then only at their level?

Or do we dare to be an eagle? Eagles are birds that are noticed, not because they are noisy or because of the splendour of their plumage but because they have learnt to fly beautifully. It is the quality of their flight that makes the impact.

Eagles have learnt to use the wind to their advantage. They know how to use even the slightest breath, and often they don't even need to flap their wings, but let the wind carry them. Wings outspread, they circle high, viewing things from a different perspective to that seen by other birds that are used to flying lower down.

'Those who wait for the Lord shall renew their strength, they shall mount up with wings like eagles' (Isaiah 40:31).

Wings like an eagle—that's what God wants for us. Learn to soar a little higher each day—heaven bound!

✥

Hagar

Recently I took my mother to a doctor's appointment. Afterwards we thought about the best way to get back to her house, as the road was closed while work was in progress to strengthen a weak bridge. We knew it was possible to get there from another direction and so we decided to try the alternative route.

We soon found ourselves trying to negotiate a maze of winding country lanes—not easy when neither of us recognized any of the village names appearing on the signposts.

Once, Mum was convinced she remembered driving home via a certain village but when we got there we found that the road went nowhere else. It was a dead end. The village was an idyllic place with thatched cottages and even a duck pond. But it wasn't where we wanted to go!

Being confused, being lost. Sometimes circumstances overwhelm us and we just don't know which way to turn.

Hagar's situation was a difficult one. Her mistress Sarah had been so desperate for a child she had decided to take matters into her own hands. Sarah took her slave girl Hagar and gave her as a wife to her husband Abram (Genesis 16:3).

However, when Sarah's plan succeeded and Hagar became pregnant, Sarah wasn't pleased at all—in fact, quite the reverse. She treated Hagar so harshly that Hagar felt she had to run away. She couldn't stand the situation any more.

It was all so unfair. Hagar had only done as her mistress ordered, and look what had happened. Here she was out in the wilderness, the last place she wanted to be. Surely this was even worse than being a slave.

Did anyone care about her desperate situation? Did anyone care how miserable she was or how she was suffering through no fault of her own?

Where was God in all this? Had he abandoned her too?

Far from it. The angel of the Lord sought out Hagar in the wilderness and asked her a very interesting question: 'Hagar... where have you come from and where are you going?' (Genesis 16:8).

Sometimes as we journey through our Christian life it might be good to ask ourselves the same question. Where have we come from?

What were the dreams God placed in your heart? Have you fulfilled them or are you in the process of doing so?

Where are we going? Have we lost our way, perhaps taken what appeared to be a shortcut, only to find that we're hopelessly off track? Have we got stuck on a roundabout where we can't seem to find the right exit?

Have we lost our way? Hagar had.

Hagar had forgotten that she was no longer just a slave. She was going to be the mother of a child who would have Abram for a father, and God had promised Abram that his offspring would be as numerous as the stars in the heavens.

Are we moving in the right direction or are we running away from God's promises, like Hagar? Do you feel that God has abandoned you?

I am sure that Hagar felt utterly alone in the wilderness. I am sure that she felt, 'Nobody cares about me', but she was wrong.

The angel of the Lord came to her in her desperate situation and gave her the directions she needed to find the way again: 'I will so greatly multiply your offspring that they cannot be counted for multitude' (Genesis 16:10).

God saw a wretched slave girl, confused, hopeless and desolate, and reminded her that her slavery was in the past. That was where she had come from but it wasn't where she was going. Her ultimate destination was no longer slavery but to be the mother of a multi-tude. What a glorious end to Hagar's journey!

Hagar called the God who met with her in that lonely wilderness place 'El-roi'—the God who sees.

God saw the suffering of a wretched slave girl bullied by her mistress and came to her at her point of need.

He sees when we are hurt and lonely.

He sees when we are struggling with difficult circumstances.

He sees when there are times of sorrow—and times of joy!

He sees and he comes to us in love, seeking us out in the wilderness and setting us gently back on the right track.

Where have you come from? Where are you going?

Have you lost your way, forgotten who you are meant to be in God? Is it time to get back on the right track?

❖

New directions

As a family, we have moved several times, but probably the most challenging was the move we made from Streatham in London to Merseyside when our oldest son was just eighteen months old.

For weeks we had been sorting and packing, and cardboard boxes were piled high in every room. One part of me felt excited at the thought of going somewhere different, but another part felt sadness at leaving so many good friends and our local church.

It was all a bit of an emotional rollercoaster and sometimes it was hard not to worry.

'What will it be like? Supposing I don't fit in…'

'Will I make new friends to replace the ones I have here?'

'Will my little boy settle?'

Although we felt sure God was in the whole thing, it was still a wrench when the time came to lock the door for the last time and set out for our new home in a part of the country we didn't know at all and where we knew nobody.

Acclimatizing took quite some time as we discovered that a few hundred miles made a surprising amount of difference. People even talked differently up there! When we asked the way to Thornton Hough (pronouncing Hough as 'how'), they just shook their heads in bewilderment: 'Never heard of it.' Only later did we discover that Hough was pronounced 'huff'!

At times I really felt that I could have done with a phrase book—and this was only another part of England. For example, to me, 'made up' meant somebody with make-up on, but to my new friends it meant 'thrilled to bits'!

Moving from the south to the north, we experienced a degree of culture shock, but for Ruth, a Moabite, moving to a different country altogether, the sense of being uprooted must have been much stronger (Ruth 1).

It had been a tragic time. Naomi's husband had died first, and then her two sons, the husbands of Orpah and Ruth. Now Naomi was going back to Israel, her homeland.

After a tearful farewell, Orpah decided to return to her own people and her own gods. Ruth chose differently. She would go with Naomi.

Ruth was going to a new country. She had no blood relatives there. The only person she knew was her mother-in-law. Probably the customs too were very different from those she was used to.

She could have stayed with her family in the land she knew already. She could have gone back to worshipping in the old way, but having experienced a different way of life, Ruth found that she did not want to return to what she had known before. She wanted to move on, to follow God wherever he led—even if that meant leaving everything else behind.

So she set out for the unknown, a place she had never been to. I am sure Ruth's friends tried to put her off.

'Why do you want to go when everything you need is here?'

'How will you manage to live? You're two women on your own. What about finance?'

'They're different from us. You won't be happy there.'

Ruth had her answer. She was going away from everything she knew, but it didn't matter because someone was going on ahead of her, someone who would take better care of her than any friend or even her parents, someone she had learned to love and trust—'the Lord, the God of Israel, under whose wings you have come for refuge' (Ruth 2:12).

Changing directions can be scary. Perhaps you are in a place where the course of your life is changing, maybe in undertaking a new project that you feel will stretch you to the utmost, a job or house move, or even in some radical alteration to your way of life.

Moving on is a challenge, but we don't need to be fearful if God is in it. 'For surely I know the plans I have for you, says the Lord, plans for your welfare and not for harm, to give you a future with hope' (Jeremiah 29:11). Wherever God wants us is ultimately the safest place to be.

When Floyd and Sally McClung of Youth With a Mission were about to move in Holland, they were actively looking for the place where God wanted them to be. And they found it—right in the heart of Amsterdam's red light district.

The red light district! How could anyone in their right minds move there with a young family to raise? How could they even consider it?

When most families move house, they ask questions like, 'Is there a garden for the kids to play in? Are the neighbours nice? Are there good schools? What's the neighbourhood like?'

The close proximity of sex shops, and prostitutes for neighbours, would not rank highly in most people's list of desirable requirements, but this is exactly what the McClungs found when they moved in. From a human point of view, such an environment would never be considered ideal family-rearing territory. The temptation to put family first and protect their children must have been strong.

Floyd and Sally could easily have opted out—it would have been an entirely natural decision and nobody would have blamed them for making it—but there was something else going on in their life. They had a strong sense of the calling of God and it was this that strengthened them in their decision to go ahead.

Because the red light district was God's choice, it was the choice of Floyd and Sally McClung, and God rewarded their obedience by richly blessing them as they shared their faith with pimps, prostitutes and drug addicts.

Ruth too was not afraid to move in obedience to God. She left her home and family, all that she was used to, putting God first in her life—and found blessing.

In fact, Ruth became part of the lineage of the Lord Jesus himself (Matthew 1:5–16), all because she was willing to follow God— wherever he led.

God of the unexpected

How do we cope with the unexpected? What happens when we are asked to provide a meal and a bed for the night without prior notice, or to cope with an extra work demand for which we weren't prepared? Do we take it in our stride or do we fall apart?

What about when it is God himself who interrupts our routines? God will use the most surprising ways to get us to become aware of him.

It's not always as dramatic as the burning bush that he used to grab Moses' attention in the desert (Exodus 3:2–4). It can actually be something very ordinary like a news broadcast, a conversation with a friend or even a library book. God once spoke to me very clearly through a plastic carrier bag!

It was during a difficult period in my life when our youngest son had a serious illness and I was virtually housebound. I went through a period of great stress and loneliness, and one day cried out to God in desperation, 'Lord, I need to know how you feel about me.'

If I had thought about it I would have expected God to speak to me through the 'normal' channels—perhaps through a Bible passage or when I was praying or even through the sermon on a Sunday.

Oddly enough, I wasn't expecting to hear from him in a secular context, and when he did, it blew my mind.

God loves to spring surprises on us to jolt us out of our pre-conceived notions of him and how he works. We might think that God would not be particularly interested in salvaging a wedding party — surely that would be beneath his notice. But the God who made the universe is also the God who turned the water into wine at Cana (John 2:1–11).

God spoke to me through an everyday situation when I wasn't expecting it at all, and it came as both shock that he could speak through something so ordinary and delight that he cared so much that he would arrange this 'coincidence' to bless me.

I'd bought a few secondhand books from the local charity shop and it was only later, when I was unwrapping them from the bag that the assistant had given me, that something stopped me in my tracks.

I suddenly realized that the carrier bag had a boldly printed slogan which read 'CLB [my initials]—Simply The Best!' What was even more precious was the overwhelming sense of God's love that I felt as I read these words.

We can dismiss incidents like this as 'lucky coincidences' but I don't think they are. How many times have you found that there has been an unexpected meeting or an unexpected happening that can only be explained by God's intervention?

Why do we have such difficulty in believing that God, who set the planets in the sky, can break into our lives in surprising and unusual ways?

Sometimes we struggle with the unexpected because we think we know what we should be doing in a given situation, and then God comes along and asks us to change direction totally or act in a way that doesn't come naturally to us.

As rational human beings we can almost experience a sense of, 'But you just can't do it like that! You're breaking every rule in the rule book!' But God invented the rule book in the first place!

It can't have been easy being a soldier in the Israelite army at the time of the battle of Jericho. After all, they had a macho image to keep up, and what was God's battle plan? Walking round the city walls seven times behind a bunch of trumpet-blowing priests! (Joshua 6:1–20).

No war commander would have used this as a military strategy for conquering an enemy force. It went against everything they'd ever been taught. The thing was that it actually worked, and because the outcome was totally unexpected it was all the more obvious that God was in charge.

God's ways are definitely not our ways, and this means that we have to be on the lookout for him turning up in the most unexpected places and in the most unlikely guises. We have to learn to turn aside when we see that burning bush, to take our shoes off and recognize that we are standing on holy ground.

Perhaps you bump into that neighbour you've been praying for; or you see an unexpected opportunity to do something for God and feel a sudden rush in your spirit that says, 'Yes, I can do this. This is for me.' These are not coincidences—they are 'God-incidences'.

Rather than letting an unexpected encounter make us falter and become flustered, we can choose instead to see it as a window of opportunity and a chance to grow in God.

Moses could have turned a blind eye to the burning bush. He could have said to himself, 'Well, I'm here to tend sheep, not to look at burning bushes', but he would have missed an incredible opportunity to meet with the living God.

Of course, the most unexpected thing of all was Jesus. The Jewish people knew that a Messiah was coming to save them but they expected him to be a great warrior or a political figure.

Never in their wildest dreams would they have seen the cross as the instrument of salvation, not just for the Jewish nation, but for the whole world. So painful. So cruel. And yet so beautiful.

Are we prepared for the unexpectedness of God? We should be. The unexpected can be scary, painful or a moment of joy—an experience that moulds us, makes us, stretches us, challenges us, excites us, reaffirms us, and encourages us—a moment that God can use.

✣

Walking the tightrope

To walk a tightrope, you have to be a little bit crazy. After all, who in their right mind would choose to venture out on a thin line suspended above a dangerous drop?

It doesn't look easy either. There are times when the tightrope walker wobbles precariously from side to side, almost losing his or her balance before once more advancing, step by careful step, until the safety of the opposite platform is reached.

Walking a tightrope is not everybody's cup of tea, but if you are a Christian, God will probably ask you to do just that at some point—to launch out from your safety platform and follow him out into the unknown.

The tightrope God calls us to walk may require us to do things that we regard as embarrassing, difficult or even dangerous. It may affect the way we see ourselves or the way that others see us. We may face rejection, misunderstanding and criticism even from those closest to us.

For Queen Esther, the tightrope was a particularly significant one and involved life-or-death choices. Should she walk the dangerous tightrope of faith or should she opt to stay on solid ground in the comfortable safety of her royal position?

Esther had everything to lose. She was queen to King Ahasuerus, the rich and powerful ruler of the Medes and Persians, but she knew only too well that her rank would not protect her from the king's anger if she offended him.

After all, she had taken the place of her predecessor, the beautiful Vashti, who had unwisely scorned the king's command. Esther knew just how easy it would be to share Vashti's fate—to be banished from the court or even lose her life.

Was it worth it? Here she had a life of luxury, richly decorated apartments, elegant clothing, sumptuous food, and servants to obey her every wish. She was the queen, holding an enviable position of power and authority.

Of course Esther had heard of the royal edict to destroy the Jewish people, a plot hatched by the scheming Haman, who hated Esther's adoptive father Mordecai and the nation to which he belonged (Esther 3:5–6). However, there was no need for her to get involved, because nobody within the palace knew that she too worshipped the God of Israel.

Mordecai had told Esther to keep her nationality a secret so that she would almost certainly be safe even if the rest of her people outside the palace walls were slaughtered. Even if the truth were discovered, probably no one would dare to lay a finger on her. She was the queen and had the king's protection.

Esther could easily have remained a bystander. Wasn't God in control? He didn't need her. Events would take their course without her intervention.

Meanwhile she could try on new garments, bathe and perfume her body, take life easily, surrounded by her entourage of willing slaves. After all, what could she possibly do?

Instead of safety, however, Esther chose to take a risk. She listened to Mordecai's wise words: 'Who knows? Perhaps you have come to royal dignity for just such a time as this' (Esther 4:14). Esther determined to use the situation in which she found herself, to be bold for God.

First, she set aside three days of fasting for the Jewish people, herself and her maids as preparation for what lay ahead. Wisely, she did business with God before doing business with the king.

The moment of truth came. To approach the king without being summoned into his presence could easily result in death, but Esther was prepared to lay her life on the line to intercede for her people, to venture out on to that tightrope. 'I will go to the king, though it is against the law; and if I perish, I perish' (Esther 4:16).

Esther's faith was rewarded when King Ahasuerus held out the golden sceptre, and her willingness to risk everything eventually resulted in an amazing defeat of Haman and his evil schemes.

Haman died on the gallows he had constructed for Mordecai, and the day of slaughter planned by him became instead a day of victory in which Esther's people triumphed over their enemies.

If Esther hadn't been prepared to step out in boldness and faith, the story might have ended very differently, but she chose to take the risk, putting her own life in the balance.

How far will we go to do God's will? Will we take risks for him? What lengths are we prepared to go to in order to stand out as Christians, disregarding the voices that say, 'Only an idiot would get up on to that piece of wire. Look how thin it is—it can't be very strong. Are you sure it will bear your weight? Don't make a spectacle of yourself!'

Christian life is radical. God is calling us to live dangerously, to be salt, to be light, to walk that tightrope for him.

According to the thesaurus, another word for 'risk' is 'opportunity'. Are we fully using the opportunities we have for God? Do we trust him enough to allow him to use us to our fullest capacity, to serve the purpose of God in our generation as Esther did?

The first time we trust ourselves entirely to God and begin to walk the narrow tightrope of faith, it is terrifying. The ground beneath us looks very far away and at times we wobble so much that we nearly do fall off. But just ahead of us, encouraging us on, watching our every step, is Jesus himself, and if we keep our eyes firmly fixed on him we will be safe.

Then an amazing thing happens. As we walk the tightrope again and again, our feet no longer fumble and keeping our balance becomes easier and easier.

Instead of worrying about what we are doing we may even find that we have acquired a taste for tightrope walking, the excitement that only comes when we are prepared to risk everything for our risen Lord!

Is anything too hard for the Lord?

The very word 'Lord' means the one who rules over all things. Our problems begin when we forget who the Lord is and that he is in control of our lives—not the politicians, not the media bosses, not the scientific brains, and certainly not ourselves.

We live in a world where everything is based on cause-and-effect principles, and so we often have problems remembering that, as Christians, we are meant to live in a whole different dimension. In a sense, we truly are strangers in this world because we are operating, or should be, by a totally different rule book.

In earthly terms it is impossible for a woman of 99 to bear a child, for a donkey to speak words of wisdom, or for a leper to be made completely whole, but in God's world that is nothing out of the ordinary.

Unfortunately it is difficult not to take on the influences of the familiar culture that has surrounded us from the day we were born. We find it only too easy to concern ourselves only with what we know can be possible, and forget that God is actually the God of the impossible.

In our minds we replace the God who can do the impossible with a God who can operate within the realms of feasibility—a God that we feel comfortable with.

With our lips we say, 'Of course we believe God can do anything' but our hearts add '…within reason'. We can ask this God to heal our neighbour's cold, but when it comes to a cancerous tumour our faith falls down.

We often admire people who possess the ability to stay level-headed, not going overboard, treading the middle path. As Christians, however, we need to learn to be unreasonable, to expect to see the Red Sea parting and the dry land appearing, rather than working out how to build a bridge to cross it.

The real question we need to face is, 'How big is our God and how far are we prepared to trust him?'

The Bible tells us that we have a God who is able to do 'abundantly far more than all we can ask or imagine' (Ephesians 3:20), but we don't always act as if that is the God in whom we believe.

The prayers we pray are often prayers that do not really stretch us. We don't ask for too much, and even when we do, we have little expectation that God will answer us. We hold back and pray 'safe' prayers so that we won't be too disappointed if nothing actually happens.

Yes, we'll pray for the little things, but what about the things we can't solve, humanly speaking: the relationship that has broken down; the tragedy that has occurred in our life; the hurts that seem as if they will never be healed; the illness that restricts us so greatly.

Why is it so hard for us to believe that the God who creates a sublime range of ice-capped mountains, and yet also designs snowflakes so that no two are ever the same, can intervene in our situation? He is an infinite God, yet one who is intimately concerned with the smallest details.

Jesus promises, 'If in my name you ask me for anything, I will do it' (John 14:14). We have only to ask and expect to hear from God.

We need to stop worrying about the why, the where, the what, the which and the how. We have a 'who' who deeply cares about us.

'I am,' says God, not 'I could be if I wanted to' or 'I might be if I felt like it.'

'I am the God who heals you' (Exodus 15:26).

'I am the God who provides for you' (Genesis 22:14).

'I am the God who sings over you with love' (Zephaniah 3:17).

In Matthew 19:26 we read, 'For mortals it is impossible, but for God all things are possible'—not some things, or just a few things, but *all* things.

That is the God we have. God of the impossible? No, a God of the infinitely possible, a God who will move the mountains but will yet respond to the tentative touch of budding faith, of the woman reaching out to touch the hem of his garment (see Luke 8:44).

Reach out with the hand of faith and touch the God who loves you. He is the answer.

✣

Coming as a child

'Truly I tell you, whoever does not receive the kingdom of God as a little child will never enter it' (Mark 10:15).

What does Jesus mean? How can I possibly become a child again? I'm an adult. Surely God isn't asking me to revert to the behaviour of a six-year-old. That would just be silly.

So what is God saying? Just for a minute, step back into childhood and see the world through a child's eyes. Children have a vulnerability and an openness, a capacity for instantly accepting things that adults struggle to come to terms with.

Children have no problem with the raising of Jairus' daughter or with Jesus walking on the water. Of course Jesus can do it. He can do anything! Faith for them is simple and uncomplicated. For us, it can be very difficult to make that leap of trust. After all, a dead person is dead; and water isn't solid, so how can you walk on it?

The mindset of an adult is often limiting when it comes to the things of God. In this case, older is not necessarily wiser! We can learn so much from children if only we are willing.

Children have an entirely different approach to many things, and often their behaviour is so much more aligned to Kingdom principles than our own. How easily they forgive when someone has wronged them. How willing they are to say 'sorry'.

Strangely, although as adults we train our children to say 'sorry' quickly, we sometimes find it very hard to practise what we preach, to humble ourselves and admit that we are in the wrong.

Another way in which children differ from adults is in their capacity to love with no strings attached and with no holding back. As adults, many of us find it hard to give ourselves to the same extent, always wary of giving too much away in case we get hurt in the process. Jesus wants us to be free of those restrictions, to love him unreservedly and to accept his love unreservedly—as a child does.

The other day, visiting friends for tea, I watched a young child squeal with delight as her father threw her up in the air and then caught her again in his waiting hands. What a picture of fatherhood!

The little girl obviously trusted her father implicitly. She never thought for one moment that he might drop her. Put an adult in the child's place, and probably the experience would be approached from a totally different angle.

'Oh no, he's going to let me go in a minute! I'm not sure whether I can cope with this. I'll be up there and he'll be down there, nothing holding me, no security, and there's no guarantee I won't hit the floor. Or I might bump my head on the ceiling if he throws me too high. Either way I'm almost certain to get hurt.

'Who's to say that he's actually going to catch me? I know he said he would but he might not. I'm not absolutely sure he will. Supposing the phone rings and he gets distracted. Then where will I be?

'How good a catcher is he, anyway? How many times has he done this before? I need proof that he can catch me—lots of it! I'm afraid...'

In contrast, the child simply waits for the moment when the father's hand releases her and enjoys the whole experience of being in mid-air without support.

She has no doubt at all that her father's hands are outstretched ready to break her fall, and excitedly demands a repeat performance for as long as the dad is able to keep it up, demonstrating absolute trust in the one who loves her.

When the wheel of her doll's pushchair breaks, I see the same child run to her dad and ask him to fix it, full of confidence that he will be able to make it as good as new. 'My dad can fix anything!' There's no hanging on to it, thinking that she can do the job better herself, or even hiding it away because she's ashamed it got broken in the first place. No, she brings it in the assurance that this is the person to come to, to get things mended.

If only we were like that with our heavenly Father, for this is what God wants most of all—not for us to be childish, but to be child-like in our relationship with him, trusting absolutely in his love and in his care for us—Abba Father, Daddy.

There's a beautiful passage in Hosea 11:3–4 where God expresses his love in the imagery of a loving parent and child:

It was I who taught Ephraim to walk,
I took them up in my arms…
I led them with cords of human kindness, with bands of love.
I was to them like those who lift infants to their cheeks.
I bent down to them and fed them.

Let us make no mistake. We are the precious objects of God's affections. We love him because he first loved us, before we ever knew him.

He will not fail us or forsake us, and his arms are outstretched, ready to catch us and hold us in his loving embrace. Loved with a Father's love to all eternity.

❖

Conclusion

She was just an ordinary woman until he came on the scene
And his love showed her all that she was meant to be.
He knew all about her, every weakness, every strength,
But that just made him love her even more,
Especially when she tried to change and grow for his sake.
Each day she learned a little more about him
And trusted him a little more,
Learned to follow where he led
And listen when he spoke.
Learned to see herself not just as part of the wallpaper
But a living stone created for a purpose,
Unique because that was the way God had designed her
And only she could fill the special place prepared for her.
No longer ordinary, but extraordinary in him
Because that was how he was
And something of him now shone in her.

Day by Day with God

You may be interested to know that BRF publishes a series of daily Bible reading notes written especially by women for women. *Day by Day with God* is published three times a year, in January, May and September. Edited by Mary Reid, the team of contributors includes Diana Archer, Beryl Adamsbaum, Fiona Barnard, Celia Bowring, Anne Coomes, Molly Dow, Rosemary Green, Margaret Killingray, Jennifer Rees Larcombe, Chris Leonard, Hilary McDowell, Kristina Petersen, Christine Platt, Elaine Pountney, Wendy Pritchard, Christina Rees, Elizabeth Rundle, Alie Stibbe, Ann Warren and Sandra Wheatley.

To subscribe to *Day by Day with God*, please complete the form below and return it to BRF with your payment.

Day by Day with God Subscriptions

Please send *Day by Day with God* to the address given below for one year, beginning with the next January / May / September issue: (delete as applicable)

	UK	Surface	Air Mail
Day by Day with God	❏ £12.15	❏ £13.50	❏ £15.75
2-year subscription	❏ £20.40	N/A	N/A

Please complete the payment details below and send your coupon, with appropriate payment, to BRF, First Floor, Elsfield Hall, 15–17 Elsfield Way, Oxford OX2 8FG

Your name _____

Your address _____

_____

_____ Postcode _____

Total enclosed £ _____ (cheques should be made payable to 'BRF')

Payment by: cheque ❏ postal order ❏ Visa ❏ Mastercard ❏ Switch ❏

Card no.

Card expiry date [ ][ ][ ][ ]   Issue number (Switch) [ ][ ][ ][ ]

Signature _____

(essential if paying by credit/Switch card)

NB: These notes are also available from Christian bookshops everywhere.

❏ Please do not send me further information about BRF publications